T0161386

THE SCROLLS OF
BISHOP TIMOTHEOS

TEXTS FROM EXCAVATIONS

EDITED BY T. G. H. JAMES

FIRST MEMOIR

THE SCROLLS OF BISHOP TIMOTHEOS

TWO DOCUMENTS FROM MEDIEVAL NUBIA

BY

J. MARTIN PLUMLEY

EGYPT EXPLORATION SOCIETY

3 DOUGHTY MEWS, LONDON WC1N 2PG

1975

LONDON

SOLD AT

THE OFFICES OF THE EGYPT EXPLORATION SOCIETY

3 *Doughty Mews, London* WC1N 2PG

*Printed in Great Britain
at the University Press, Oxford
by Vivian Ridler
Printer to the University*

FOREWORD

THE Scrolls of Bishop Timotheos found in January 1964 at the Fortress of Qaṣr Ibrîm in Nubia must be reckoned amongst the most important discoveries in a very successful season's work by the Egyptian Exploration Society, whose excavations there formed part of the British contribution to the UNESCO Campaign to save the Nubian Monuments.

In the first place these Scrolls from Nubia are without question the finest surviving examples of medieval Letters Testimonial issued by a Patriarch of the Coptic Church to a bishop after his consecration and before his subsequent enthronement in his own Cathedral Church. These documents are also valuable witnesses to the antiquity of the practice of issuing such letters, and, since they are dated, they are an aid to palaeographical studies. But by far their greatest importance lies in the fact that they provide indisputable evidence that the Christian Church was still surviving in Lower Nubia in the late fourteenth century, and that its adherents were numerous enough to warrant the continued provision of a bishop to care for them. Certain features in the burial of Bishop Timotheos suggest that the times were troubled ones for the Church. It would seem that his tenure of the See of Nubia was short, his death sudden and possibly violent, and his burial secret and hasty. That Nubia was in an unsettled state in the last half of the fourteenth century is indicated by the fact that the enthronement of Timotheos was performed in Upper Egypt, and not, as might have been expected, in his Cathedral Church at Qaṣr Ibrîm. Though excavations on the site have not revealed the physical remains of any successors to Bishop Timotheos, there is some evidence from written sources found on Qaṣr Ibrîm to suggest that he was not the last of the bishops of Nubia and that there were Christians in some strength still occupying the place in the second half of the fifteenth century. Indeed, it is possible that they may have continued there until the Fortress was taken over by the Bosnian mercenaries sent thither by the Sultan Süleyman the Magnificent in A.D. 1528.

It had been my intention to publish these Scrolls as soon as possible after their discovery, but a number of circumstances, not least the need to press on with field work at Qaṣr Ibrîm as intensively as possible because of the threat posed to the site by the steady rise of the Nile waters, have delayed me more than I could have wished. The present edition of the texts of the Scrolls is an attempt to place in the hands of scholars the contents of the documents in a way which I trust will be both useful and reliable. In addition to photographs each Scroll has been reproduced in a modern transcription. Translations into English of both texts is offered and a modest number of notes appended.

In the preparation of this edition of the Bishop's Scrolls I have been helped by a number of colleagues to whom I am most grateful. In Cairo Professor Murad Kamal made the first transcript of the Arabic text and provided a tentative translation. During his stay in England Abuna Shenouda of the Syrian Monastery in the Wâdi Naṭrûn made a revised translation based on photographs of the Arabic text. I am further indebted to Dr. Albert Zaki Iskander, Fellow of the Wellcome Institute of Medicine, London, and to Dr. George Bebawi, one of my research students at Cambridge, for their valuable comments on the Arabic text. A final revision of the text and the translation of the Arabic has been carried out by Dr. Martin Hinds, University Lecturer in Arabic Studies at Cambridge. Dr. Hinds has also provided a number of notes on the Arabic text. The first-hand copy of the Coptic text was made by Dr. Violet MacDermot, one of my colleagues on the 1964 Expedition. The translation of the Coptic text is my responsibility. I have deliberately tried to keep the rendering as literal as possible, in some instances at the expense of elegance. For certain improvements in the translation, for a number of valuable notes, and for help with the Greek portions of the text I am greatly indebted to Dr. James Drescher, and to Mr. T. C. Skeat. Finally I have to thank the authorities of the Egyptian Museum in Cairo for their assistance to Dr. MacDermot and myself in photographing and recording the Scrolls. Nor must I fail to express my thanks to Dr. Zaki Iskander and his staff at the laboratory of the Egyptian Museum for their help, and, in particular, to congratulate them on the successful outcome of their work in unrolling and conserving the two Scrolls of Bishop Timotheos. They now bear the Cairo numbers 90223 (Coptic) and 90224 (Arabic).

J. MARTIN PLUMLEY

Selwyn College
Cambridge
September 1970

CONTENTS

PART 1

INTRODUCTION

INTRODUCTION

The Finding of the Scrolls

ON the morning of Monday, 6 January 1964 the workmen who were clearing the debris from the stairway leading to the North Crypt of the Cathedral Church of Qaṣr Ibrîm, came upon a burial lying a short distance under the arched entrance to the crypt. Examination of the burial *in situ* quickly revealed that it was a Christian interment. The body was then removed carefully to the nave of the Cathedral for more detailed examination. This examination established that the burial was that of a high-ranking ecclesiastic, who had been buried under a linen shroud in his ordinary outdoor garb. The presence of a fine wrought-iron benedictional cross lying on the breast of the body indicated that the owner was a bishop. Any doubt on this identification was removed by the discovery under the body, slightly to the left side, of two large paper Scrolls, which had been concealed there at the time of burial.

Since the paper of the Scrolls was in a very brittle condition and showed signs of having been attacked by insects, no attempt was made at unrolling them. On the recommendation of Dr. Zaki Iskander of the Egyptian Antiquities Service, who was in Nubia at that time and who made a special visit to Qaṣr Ibrîm to advise on the preservation of the Scrolls, each Scroll was moistened slightly in steam and then placed in an air-tight plastic bag, pending their transport (by air under the charge of Mr. Aly El Khouli, the Expedition's Inspector) to the Laboratory of the Egyptian Museum in Cairo.

Description of the Scrolls

As the result of the painstaking and careful work carried out at Cairo by Dr. Zaki Iskander and his colleagues in the Laboratory both Scrolls were successfully unrolled. Each Scroll proved to be no less than $482\pm$ cm. in length and 34 cm. in width. Each Scroll had been constructed by the gumming together of ten sheets of paper, each $49\pm$ cm. in length. The overlaps of each of the nine joins average $1\cdot4\pm$ cm. The surface of the paper had been treated originally by a wash of some resinous substance. Though both Scrolls had been attacked by insects and there are some patches of discoloration, the damage to the writing, apart from one passage, is fortunately slight.

One Scroll is written in the Bohairic dialect of Coptic, the other is in Arabic. It is to be noted that the Coptic Scroll contains a few lines of Greek. Though each document is the counterpart of the other, nevertheless there are a number of differences in wording.

The contents of each Scroll are headed by the representation of an ornamental cross in black, red, yellow, and green. Though both crosses are based on the same design, that in the Coptic Scroll is more elaborate and finer in execution. Both crosses are surrounded by a number of monograms, and both have the Greek title ZYΛωN (*sic*) ZωHC 'tree of life'. It is noticeable that in the Arabic Scroll all the monograms are Greek in origin, whereas in the other Scroll the monograms are Coptic in origin.

The main body of the text consists of 166 lines in the Coptic Scroll and fifty-eight lines in the Arabic. The Coptic Scroll commences with eleven lines of large ornamental letters, eight lines in black, and three in red. These introductory lines are followed by a single line of highly ornamental

Arabic which is followed by a single line of Coptic letters in a hand which might seem to imitate the flowing ornamental Arabic which precedes. These two lines are flanked on each side by an elongated ornament. Seven lines of the large ornamental Coptic hand follow, all but the sixth being in black ink. The sixth is in red. In the Arabic Scroll the identical ornamental Arabic and Coptic lines appear (ll. 1–4 on p. 29), likewise flanked on each side by elongated ornaments, but in this case preceded by two lines of large Arabic characters. It is to be noted that of the fifty-eight lines of Arabic only one, the sixth, is written in red ink.

Contents of the Scrolls

Each Scroll contains a Letter Testimonial (ΕΠΙСΤΟΛΗ СΥСΤΑΤΙΚΗ. Arab. Taqlîd) from the Patriarch Gabriel IV (A.D. 1370–8) to the people of Nubia informing them that he had consecrated for them a new bishop, Timotheos, in the place of their deceased bishop, Athanasios, and instructing them to receive and enthrone Timotheos in his see.[1]

At the end of each Scroll are the autograph witnesses of the bishops who were present at the rites and ceremonies performed on behalf of the newly consecrated bishop. Two of the witnessing bishops were present at his consecration and two at his subsequent enthronement. In the Coptic Scroll the autographs are written in Coptic, and in the Arabic Scroll in Arabic. An interesting addition to the Coptic witnesses is a passage in passable Greek by the hand of the fourth bishop. Unfortunately there are a number of lacunae in this passage, which have been caused by holes in the paper at this point.

When the Scrolls were first rolled up, brief notes in Arabic were placed along the outer edge of each document. These notes are now difficult to read because of some damage to the outer edges and because the ink is much faded. Before unrolling it was possible to read the words, 'By the hand of the Fatherly Patriarch Gabriel of the great city of Alexandria'. But since the mounting of the Scrolls under glass it is more difficult to read the notes, which have been obscured by the edges of the wooden frames in which the documents are now preserved.

Finally, on the back of the Arabic Scroll, about 20 cm. from the top edge are the remains of seven lines containing a rough but incomplete table of dates (cf. p. 41, Pl. XXIV).

---

[1] Dr. G. H. Bebawi kindly drew my attention to a fourteenth-century manuscript in the Bibliothèque Nationale at Paris (Arab. 203) which contains an exemplar for such letters. On the Taqlîd, cf. W. E. Crum, *PSBA*, 20, 270 ff.

For the rite of the Institution of a Bishop in his Cathedral, cf. R. Tuki, ⲡⲓⲭⲱⲙ ⲉϥⲉⲣⲁⲡⲁⲛⲧⲟⲕⲧⲓⲛ ⲉϫⲉⲛⲡⲓⲉⲩⲭ ⲏ ⲉⲑⲟⲩⲁⲃ (Rome, 1761), vol. i. 113, 230, 245, 261; H. Denzinger, *Ritus orientalium* (Würzburg, 1864), ii. 33; E. Renaudot, *Liturgiarum orientalium collectio* (Paris, 1716), i. 494; P. J. Vansleb, *Histoire de l'église d'Alexandrie* (Paris, 1677), 163.

PART 2

THE COPTIC SCROLL

(Cairo 90223)

ϩⲉⲛⲥⲫⲣⲁⲛ ⲙ̅ⲫⲓⲱⲧ
ⲛⲉⲙⲡⲓϣⲏⲣⲓ ∴ ⲛⲉⲙⲡⲓⲡ̅ⲛ̅ⲁ̅
ⲉ̀ⲑⲟⲩⲁⲃ ⲉ̀ⲟⲩⲛⲟ̅ϯⲛⲟⲩⲱⲧ

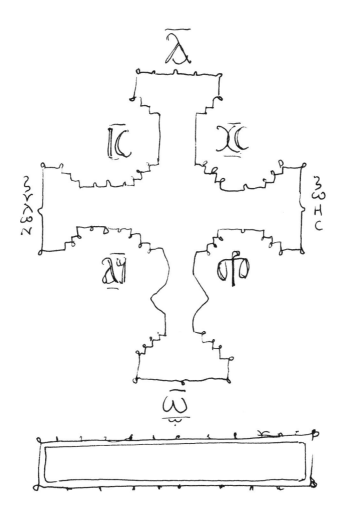

ΤΟΙϹ ΤΑΠΑΝΤΑ ΤΟ ΥΘΕΟΥ   (Red)

ΦΙΛΟ ΧΥ ΤΑ ΤΩ ΠΡ ΕϹΒΥ

ΤΕΡΟΥ ΔΙΑΚΟΝΟΥ ΥΠΟ

ΔΙΑΚΟΝΟΥ ΑΝΑΓ ΝΩϹ

5 ΤΟΝ ΨΑΛΜΟΤΟΝ ΤΑΑΛΩ

ΤΗϹ ΠΟΛΙϹ ΠΧ ΩΡΑϹ ΝΕΜ ΤΛΥ Β Η   (Red)

ΤΟΝ ΟΜΑ Α Υ ΤΗϹ ΑΓΠΗ ΤΟΝ

ΠΝΑ ΤΙΚΟΝ ΔΕΚΝΟΙϹ ΑΒΒΑ

ΓΑΒΡΙΗΛ ΝΚΥ ΠΑΤΗΡ ΧΕΡ ΕΙΝ

10 ΓΑΒΡΙΗΛ ΦΒΩΚ ΝΙΗϹ ΠΧϹ

ϨΕΝΠΙϹΜΟ Τ Ν ΤΕ ΦΤ   (Red)

Glory be to God always and for ever (in Arabic)

ΠΙΩΟΥ ΦΑ ΦΤ ΠΕ

ΝΕΜ ΝΕΥϨΑΠ ΝΑΤΥΤΑϨΩΟΥ

15 ΠΙΑΡΧΗΕΠΙϹΚΟΠΟϹ ΝΤΕ ΤΝΙϢ

Τ ΜΠΟΛΙϹ ΡΑΚΟΤ ΝΕΜ ΒΑΒΥ

ΛΩΝ ΝΕΜ ΝΕϹ ΘΩϢ ΝΕΜ ΤΛΥ

ΒΗ ΝΕΜ ΝΙΕΘΑΥϢ ΝΕΜ ΝΗ ΕΤΕ

ΝΟΥΟΥ ΝΕΜ Ε ΜΒΑΚΙ ΕΤϨΕΝΠΕ   (Red)

20 ΜΕΝΤ ΝΕΜ ΦΡΙΚΙΑ

ΤΕΝΤΑΜΟΤΕ ΜΜΩΤΕΝ Ω ΝΙϢΗΡΙ ΜΜΕΝΡΑΤ   (Red)

ΜΜΑΙΧϹ ΝΟΡΘΟΔΟΞΟϹ ΝΙΚΛΗΡΙΚΟϹ   (Red)

ΝΙΠΡΕϹΒΥΤΕΡΟϹ ΝΙΔΙΑΚΟΝΟϹ ΝΕΜ ΝΙ

ΒΑΘΜΟϹ ΤΗΡΟΥ ΝΤΕ ΝΙΚΛΗΡΙΚΟϹ ΝΕΜ ΝΙ

25 ϦΕΛΛΟΙ ΝΑΡΧΩΝ ΝΕΜ ΠΙΛΑΟϹ ΤΗΡϤ Ν

ΟΡΘΟΔΟΞΟϹ ΕΤϨΕΝΠ ΘΩϢ ΝΤΠΟΛΙϹ Μ

ΜΑΙΧϹ ΠΧΩΡΑϹ ΝΕΜ ΤΛΥΒΗ ΝΕΜ ΝΕϹ

ΘΩϢ ΤΗΡΟΥ

ΦΤ ΕϤΕϹΜΟΥ ΕΡΩΟΥ ΝΤΕϤΑΡΕϨ ΕΡΩΟΥ Ν

30 ΤΕϤΘΡΕΠΟΥΑΜΑϨΙ ΜΟΥΝ ΕΒΟΛ ΝΤΕϤ

8

ⲤⲘⲞⲨ ⲈⲚⲞⲨⲘⲀⲚϢⲰⲠⲒ · Ⲉ · ⲚⲈⲘ ⲚⲞⲨϢⲎⲢⲒ ⲚⲈⲘ

ⲚⲞⲨϮⲘⲒ · Ⲉ · ⲚⲈⲘ ⲚⲞⲨⲈⲔⲔⲖⲎⲤⲒⲀ · Ⲉ · ⲚⲈⲘ ⲌⲰⲂ

ⲚⲒⲂⲈⲚ ⲈⲦⲞⲨⲈⲢⲀⲚⲈⲤⲦⲢⲈⲪⲈⲤⲐⲈ ⲚϨⲎⲦⲞⲨ

ⲒⲦⲈ ϬⲞ · Ⲉ · ⲒⲦⲈ ⲪⲢⲀⲄⲘⲀⲦⲒⲀ ⲚⲈⲘ ⲚⲞⲨⲒⲞⲠⲎ · Ⲉ ·

35 ⲚⲈⲘ ⲚⲞⲨϢⲀⲚϢ · Ⲉ · ⲚⲈⲘ ⲚⲞⲨⲬⲰⲢⲞⲤ · Ⲉ · ⲚⲦⲈϤ

ⲚⲞⲌⲈⲘ ⲚⲚⲞⲨⲮⲨⲬⲎ ϦⲈⲚⲠⲈϤϢⲰⲂϢ ⲈⲦⲬⲞⲢ

ⲚⲈⲘ ⲦⲈϤⲞⲨⲒⲚⲀⲘ ⲈⲦϬⲞⲤⲒ · Ⲉ · ⲚⲦⲈϤϮ Ⲙ̄ⲦⲞⲚ

Ⲙ̄ⲮⲨⲬⲎ ⲚⲒⲂⲈⲚ ⲈⲦⲀⲨⲤⲒⲚⲒ ⲚⲦⲰⲞⲨ · Ⲉ · ⲚⲦⲈϤ

ⲦⲎⲒⲤ ⲚⲰⲞⲨ · Ⲉ · ⲈⲒⲢⲒ Ⲛ̄ⲚⲎ ⲈⲐⲢⲀⲚⲀϤ ϦⲈⲚⲞⲨϨⲨ

40 ⲠⲞⲦⲀⲔⲎ · Ⲉ · ⲚⲦⲈϤⲦⲀϪⲢⲰⲞⲨ ⲚⲈⲘ ⲚⲞⲨⲈⲢⲎⲞⲨ

ϦⲈⲚⲞⲨⲀⲄⲀⲠⲎ · Ⲉ · ⲚⲈⲘ ϦⲈⲚⲠⲒⲚⲀϨϮ ⲚⲞⲢⲐⲞⲆⲞ

ⲌⲞⲤ ϢⲀⲠⲒⲚⲒϤⲒ Ⲛ̄ϦⲀⲈ · Ⲉ ·

ⲒⲦⲈⲚ ⲚⲒⲠⲢⲈⲤⲂⲨⲀ Ⲛ̄ⲦⲈ ϮⲐⲈⲞⲦⲞⲔⲞⲤ ⲈⲐⲞⲨⲀⲂ † ⲀⲄⲒⲀ ⲘⲀⲢⲒⲀ · Ⲉ · ⲚⲈⲘ ⲚⲒϮϨⲞ ⲚⲦⲈⲠⲈⲚⲒⲰⲦ Ⲉ

45 ⲐⲞⲨⲀⲂ ⲚⲈⲨⲀⲄⲄⲈⲖⲒⲤⲦⲎⲤ ⲘⲀⲢⲔⲞⲤ · Ⲉ · ⲚⲈⲘ ⲚⲎ

ⲈⲐⲞⲨⲀⲂ ⲦⲎⲢⲞⲨ ⲀⲘⲎⲚ · Ⲉ ·

ϦⲈⲚⲠⲒⲬⲒⲚⲐⲢⲈϤϮ ⲈⲦϬⲞⲤⲒ ⲞⲨⲰϢ ⲈⲐⲰϨⲈⲘ

ⲚⲰⲦⲈⲚ ⲚⲞⲨⲈⲠⲒⲤⲔⲞⲠⲞⲤ Ⲛ̄ⲦϤⲈⲂⲒⲰ ⲚⲀⲂⲂⲀ

ⲀⲐⲀⲚⲀⲤⲒⲞⲤ ⲠⲈⲦⲈⲚⲒⲰⲦ · Ⲉ · Π̅Ⲟ̅Ⲥ̅ ⲘⲀ Ⲙ̄ⲦⲞⲚ Ⲛ

50 ⲦⲈϤⲮⲨⲬⲎ ⲚⲈⲘ ⲚⲎ ⲈⲐⲞⲨⲀⲂ Ⲛ̄ⲦⲀⲨ ϦⲈⲚⲠⲒⲠ̂

ⲢⲀⲆⲒⲤⲞⲤ Ⲛ̄ⲦⲈⲠⲞⲨⲚⲞϤ

ⲞⲨⲞϨ ⲀϤϮⲘⲀϮ ⲈⲤⲰⲦⲠ Ⲙ̄ⲠⲒⲤⲞⲚ Ⲛ̄ⲀⲄⲀⲠⲎⲦⲞⲤ

ⲚⲈⲨⲤⲈⲂⲎⲤ Ⲙ̄ⲘⲀⲒⲬ̅Ⲣ̅Ⲥ̅ · Ⲉ · Ⲛ̄ⲀⲄⲀⲐⲞⲤ Ⲛ̄ⲢⲈⲘ

ⲢⲀⲨϢ · Ⲉ · ⲈⲦⲐⲈⲂⲒⲎⲞⲨⲦ ⲚⲤⲈⲀⲤⲒⲀ · Ⲉ · ⲪⲀⲠⲒⲌⲎ̅

55 Ⲛ̄ⲀⲦⲔⲀⲔⲒⲀ · Ⲉ · ⲪⲀⲠⲒⲠ̅Ⲛ̅Ⲁ̅ ⲈⲦⲦⲈⲚⲚⲎⲞⲨⲦ

ⲪⲎ ⲈⲦⲈⲢϨⲞϮ ϦⲀⲦϨⲎ Ⲙ̄Ⲫ̄Ϯ · Ⲉ · ⲞⲨⲞϨ ⲈⲐⲘⲞ

ϢⲒ ϦⲈⲚ ⲚⲎ ⲈⲐⲢⲀⲚⲀϤ · Ⲉ · ⲞⲨⲞϨ ⲈⲦϪⲒ ⲚⲦⲞⲦϤ

ⲈⲦⲈϤⲤⲦⲢⲀⲦⲀ ⲈⲐⲘⲈϨ Ⲛ̄ⲚⲞⲘⲞⲤ · Ⲉ · ⲚⲈⲘ ⲔⲰⲦ̄

ⲚⲈⲘ ⲠⲀⲢⲀⲆⲞⲤⲒⲤ · Ⲉ · ⲠⲒⲘⲀⲒⲬ̅Ⲣ̅Ⲥ̅ ⲚⲞⲢⲐⲞⲆⲞⲌⲞ̅Ⲥ̅

60 ⲠⲒⲠⲢⲈⲤⲂⲨⲦⲈⲢⲞⲤ · Ⲉ · ⲪⲀⲠⲒⲂⲒⲞⲤ Ⲛ̄ϢⲞⲨⲈ ⲠⲈ

ⲚⲞⲨ Ⲙ̀ⲘⲞϤ ⲦⲒⲘⲞⲐⲈⲞⲤ ⲔⲀⲦⲀⲪⲎ ⲈⲦⲈϤⲰϢ

Ⲛ̀ⲢⲀⲚ ⳼

Ⲫⲁⲓ ⲁϥϣⲱⲡⲓ Ⲛ̀ⲞⲨⲠⲢⲈⲤⲂⲨⲦⲈⲢⲞⲤ ⲞⲨⲞⳅ Ⲙ̀ⲘⲞ

ⲚⲀⲬⲞⲤ Ⲉ̀ⲬⲈⲚ ⲦⲈⲔⲔⲖⲎⲤⲒⲀ̀ Ⲛ̀ⲦⲈ Ⲧ ⲐⲈⲞⲦⲞⲔ ⲇ

65 Ⲉ̀ⲐⲞⲨⲀⲂ Ⲧⲁ̀ⲅⲒⲀ ⲘⲀⲢⲒⲀ ⲠⲬⲰⲢⲀⲤ ⲚⲈⲘ Ⲧ ⲖⲨⲂⲎ ⳾Ⲉ

Ⲟ ⲨⲞⳅ Ⲛ̀ⲀⲓϤ Ⲛ̀Ⲩ̀ⲅⲞⲨⲘⲈⲚⲞⲤ ⳾Ⲉ ⲞⲨⲞⳅ ⲀⲚⲬⲞⲔϤ

Ⲛ̀Ⲉ̀ⲠⲒⲤⲔⲞⲠⲞⲤ ⲈⲦⲈϤⲈ̀ⲠⲀⲢⲬⲒⲀ̀ Ⲉ̀ⲦⲀⲚⲈⲢϢⲞⲢⲠ

Ⲛ̀ⲦⲀⲞⲨⲈ̀ ⲠⲈⲤⲢⲀⲚ ⳾Ⲉ ⳦ⲈⲚⲠⲒⲈ̀ⳅⲞⲞⲨ Ⲛ̀ⲦⲈ Ⲧ ⲔⲨⲢⲒ

Ⲁ̀ⲔⲎ Ⲉ̀ⲦⲈⲤⲞⲨ ⲓ̅ⲑ̅ Ⲙ̀ⲠⲒⲀⲂⲞⲦ Ⲁ̀ⲐⲰⲢ ⳦ⲈⲚ Ⲧ ⲘⲀⳅ

70 ⲁ̅ⲡⲏ̅ Ⲛ̀ⲢⲞⲘⲠⲒ Ⲛ̀ⲦⲈ ⲚⲒⲀ̀ⲅⲒⲞⲤ Ⲙ̀ⲘⲀⲢⲦⲨⲢⲞⲤ ⳾Ⲉ

⳦ⲈⲚ ⲦⲚⲒϢ Ⲧ Ⲛ̀ⲈⲔⲔⲖⲎⲤⲒⲀ̀ Ⲛ̀ⲦⲈ Ⲧ ⲐⲈⲞ̀ⲦⲞⲔⲞⲤ

Ⲉ̀ⲐⲞⲨⲀⲂ Ⲧⲁ̀ⲅⲒⲀ ⲘⲀⲢⲒⲀ̀ Ⲧⲁ̀ⲚⲀⲂⲀⲆⲎ ⳦ⲈⲚⲠⲒ

ⲪⲰⲤⲦⲀⲦⲞⲚ Ⲛ̀ⲦⲈ ⲬⲎⲘⲒ ⲐⲎ ⲈⲦⲢⲰⲒⲤ ⳾Ⲉ

⳦ⲈⲚⲠⲬⲒⲚⲐⲢⲞⲨⲄⲢⲀⲞⲨ Ⲛ̀ⲬⲈ ⳅⲀⲚⲞⲨⲞⲚ Ⲛ̀ⲦⲈ ⲚⲎ

75 Ⲉ̀ⲦⲈ ⲚⲞⲨⲚ Ⲛ̀Ⲉ̀ⲠⲒⲤⲔⲞⲠⲞⲤ ⳾Ⲉ ⲚⲈⲘ ⲚⲒⲔⲖⲎⲢⲒⲔⲞⲤ

ⲚⲈⲘ ⲚⲒⳅⲈⲖⲖⲞⲒ Ⲛ̀ⲀⲢⲬⲰⲚ ⲈⲦⲦⲀⲒⲎⲞⲨⲦ ⳾Ⲉ

ⲚⲈⲘ ⲠⲒⲖⲀⲞⲤ Ⲛ̀ⲞⲢⲐⲞⲆⲞⳎⲞⲤ ⳾Ⲉ Ⲫ Ⲧ ⲈϤⲈⲤⲘⲨ

Ⲉ̀ⲢⲰⲞⲨ ⳦ⲈⲚⲤⲘⲞⲨ ⲚⲒⲂⲈⲚ Ⲛ̀Ⲉ̀ⲠⲞⲨⲢⲀⲚⲒⲞⲚ ⳾Ⲉ

Ⲟ ⲨⲞⳅ ⲀⲚⲬⲰⲔ Ⲉ̀ⲂⲞⲖ Ⲉ̀ⲬⲰϤ Ⲛ̀ⲚⲒⲀ̀ⲚⲀⲄⲚⲰⲤⲒⲤ ⳾Ⲉ

80 ⲈⲦⲤϤⲈ ⳾Ⲉ ⲚⲈⲘ Ⲧ ⲬⲒⲢⲰⲦⲞⲚⲒⲀ ⳾Ⲉ ⲞⲨⲞⳅ ⲀⲚⲈⲢ

ⲤⲦⲞⲖⲒ Ⳝ ⲒⲚ Ⲙ̀ⲘⲞϤ Ⲛ̀ⲚⲒⳅⲂⲰⲤ Ⲛ̀ⲦⲈ Ⲧ ⲘⲈⲦ

ⲞⲨⲎⲂ ⲔⲀⲦⲀ ⲠⲈⲦⲤⲈⲘⲠϢⲀ ⳾Ⲉ ⲞⲨⲞⳅ ⲀⲚ Ⲧ ⲚⲀϤ

Ⲙ̀ⲠⲒϢ ⲂⲰⲦ Ⲙ̀ⲂⲈⲚⲒⲠⲒ ⲈⲐⲢⲈϤⲘⲞⲚⲒ Ⲙ̀ⲠⲈϤ

ⲖⲀⲞⲤ ⳾Ⲉ ⳦ⲈⲚⲠⲒⲘⲀ Ⲙ̀ⲘⲞⲚⲒ ⲈⲐⲞⲨⲈⲤⲐⲰⲚ Ⲙ̀

85 ⲂⲀⲤⲒⲖⲒⲔⲞⲚ ⳾Ⲉ ⲞⲨⲞⳅ Ⲛ̀ⲦⲈϤⲀ̀ⲢⲈⳅ Ⲉ̀ⲢⲰⲞⲨ

Ⲉ̀ⲂⲞⲖ ⳅⲀⲚⲒⲞⲨⲰⲚϤ Ⲛ̀ⲢⲈϤⳅⲰⲖⲈⲘ ⳾Ⲉ ⲞⲨⲞⳅ

Ⲛ̀ⲦⲈϤⲦⲈⲘⲘⲀⳡⲞⲨ Ⲉ̀ⲂⲞⲖ ⳦ⲈⲚⲚⲈϤⲤⲂⲰⲞⲨⲒ̀

Ⲛ̀Ⲁ̀ⲠⲞⲤⲦⲞⲖⲒⲔⲞⲚ ⳾Ⲉ ⲞⲨⲞⳅ ⲀⲚⲘⲞⲨ Ⲧ ⲈⲠⲈϤ

ⲢⲀⲚ ⲀⲂⲂⲀ ⲦⲒⲘⲞⲐⲈⲞⲤ ⳾Ⲉ

90 Ⲟ ⲨⲞⳅ ⲀⲨ ⳠⲀⲤϤ Ⲉ̀ⲠϢⲰⲒ Ⲛ̀ⲬⲈ ⲪⲎ ⲈⲦ ⳠⲞⲤⲒ Ⲛ̀ⲞⲨ

10

ⲌⲎⲔⲒ ⲈⲂⲞⲖ ⲌⲀⲞⲨⲔⲞⲠⲢⲒⲀ ·ⲉ· ⲈⲐⲢⲈⲨⲌⲈⲘⲤⲒ

ⲚⲈⲘ ⲚⲒⲀⲢⲬⲰⲚ Ⲛ̇ⲦⲈⲠⲈⲨⲖⲀⲞⲤ ·ⲉ·

⊙ⲨⲞⲌ ⲀⲠⲒⲈⲢⲨⲒⲨⲒ ⲨⲰⲠⲒ ⲚⲀⲨ ⲌⲒⲦⲈⲚⲠⲒⲌⲘⲞᷘ

ⲈⲦⲀⲨⲞ̅Ⲧ̅Ⲩ ⲌⲒⲦⲈⲚⲠⲒⲠ̅Ⲛ̅Ⲁ ⲈⲐⲞⲨⲀⲂ ·ⲉ· ⲈⲐⲢⲈ|

95 ⲤⲰⲚⲌ ·ⲉ· ⲞⲨⲞⲌ Ⲛ̇ⲦⲈⲨⲂⲰⲖ Ⲉ̇ⲂⲞⲖ ⲌⲒⲦⲈⲚⲠⲒ

ⲬⲀⲬⲒ Ⲉ̇ⲬⲰⲨ ·ⲉ· ⲈⲐⲢⲈⲨⲈⲢⲀ̇ⲅⲒⲀⲌⲒⲚ Ⲛ̇ⲌⲀⲚ

ⲈⲔⲔⲖⲎⲤⲒⲀ̇ ·ⲉ· ⲚⲈⲘ ⲌⲀⲚⲐⲨⲤⲒⲀⲤⲦⲎⲢⲒⲞⲚ

Ⲙ̇ⲂⲈⲢⲒ ·ⲉ· ⲚⲈⲘ Ⲉ̇ⲪⲰⲨ Ⲛ̇ⲌⲀⲚⲔⲖⲎⲢⲒⲔⲞⲤ

Ⲛ̇ⲬⲒⲚⲬⲎ ·ⲉ· Ⲙ̇ⲪⲢⲎϮ Ⲉ̇ⲦⲀⲨϮ Ⲛ̇ⲬⲒⲚⲬⲎ ·ⲉ·

100 ⊙ⲨⲞⲌ Ⲉ̇ⲒⲢⲈ Ⲛ̇ⲌⲰⲂ ⲚⲒⲂⲈⲚ Ⲉ̇ⲦⲞⲨⲒⲢⲒ Ⲙ̇ⲘⲰⲞⲨ

Ⲛ̇ⲬⲈ ⲚⲒⲈ̇ⲠⲒⲤⲔⲞⲠⲞⲤ Ⲙ̇ⲠⲈⲨⲢⲎϮ ·ⲉ· Ⲉ̇ⲀⲚⲞⲨⲞⲢⲠᷘ

ⲌⲀⲢⲰⲦⲈⲚ ⲘⲈⲚⲈⲚⲤⲀ Ⲉ̇ⲦⲀⲨⲨⲒⲂϮ ·ⲉ· ⲞⲨⲞⲌ ⲀⲨ

ⲨⲰⲠⲒ Ⲛ̇ⲔⲈⲞⲨⲀⲒ Ⲛ̇ⲢⲰⲘⲒ Ⲙ̇ⲂⲈⲢⲒ ·ⲉ· ⲈⲨⲘⲈⲌ

Ⲉ̇ⲂⲞⲖ ⲤⲈⲚⲌⲘⲞⲦ ⲚⲒⲂⲈⲚ Ⲙ̇Ⲡ̅Ⲛ̅ⲀⲦⲒⲔⲞⲚ ·ⲉ·

105 ⲌⲒⲦⲈⲚϮⲆⲰⲢⲈⲀ Ⲉ̇ⲦⲀⲨ⳪ⲒⲦⲤ ·ⲉ· ⲚⲈⲘ ⲠⲒⲂⲀⲐⲘⲞⲤ

Ⲛ̇Ⲁ̇ⲠⲞⲤⲦⲞⲖⲒⲔⲞⲚ ⲀⲨⲈⲢⲘⲈⲦⲈⲬⲒⲚ Ⲙ̇ⲘⲞⲨ

ⲞⲨⲞⲌ ⲀⲤⲨⲰⲠⲒ Ⲉ̇ⲪⲰⲨ ⲠⲈ ·ⲉ·

ⲤⲈⲘⲠⲨⲀ ⲆⲈ ⲚⲰⲞⲨ ·ⲉ· ⲞⲨⲞⲌ ⲤⲨⲈ Ⲉ̇ⲢⲰⲞⲨ Ⲉ̇Ⲓ Ⲉ̇ⲂⲞ̊Ⲗ

ⲌⲀⲬⲰⲨ ·ⲉ· ⲞⲨⲞⲌ Ⲛ̇ⲦⲞⲨⲨⲰⲠⲨ Ⲉ̇ⲢⲰⲞⲨ Ⲏ̇ⲈⲚ

110 ⲞⲨⲦⲀⲒⲞ ⲚⲈⲘ ⲞⲨⲦⲒⲘⲎ ⲚⲈⲘ ⲞⲨⲢⲀⲨⲒ ·ⲉ· ⲚⲈⲘᷘ

ⲐⲈⲖⲎⲖ ·ⲉ· ⲚⲈⲘ Ⲉ̇ⳝⲚⲈⲬⲰⳝ ⲚⲀⲨ ·ⲉ· ⲚⲈⲘ Ⲉ̇

ⲤⲰⲦⲈⲘ Ⲛ̇ⲤⲀ ⲚⲈⲨⲤⲀⲬⲒ ⲌⲰⲤ ⲒⲰⲦ ·ⲉ· ⲞⲨⲞⲌ Ⲛ̇

Ⲥ̅Ⲥ̅ ·ⲉ· ⲞⲨⲞⲌ Ⲛ̇ⲚⲎⲂ ·ⲉ· ⲚⲈⲘ ⲞⲨⲎⲂ Ⲛ̇ⲦⲈϮ

ⲞⲨⲞⲌ Ⲛ̇ⲢⲈⲨϮⲤⲂⲰ Ⲛ̇ⲀⲄⲀⲐⲞⲤ ·ⲉ· ⲪⲎ ⲈⲦⲤⲰ

115 ⲦⲈⲘ Ⲛ̇ⲤⲰⲨ ⲀⲨⲤⲰⲦⲈⲘ Ⲛ̇ⲤⲰⲒ ·ⲉ· ⲞⲨⲞⲌ ⲪⲎ

ⲈⲦⲤⲰⲦⲈⲘ Ⲛ̇ⲤⲰⲒ ⲀⲨⲤⲰⲦⲈⲘ Ⲛ̇ⲤⲀⲠ⳧Ⲥ̅ ·ⲉ·

⊙ⲨⲞⲌ Ⲉ̇ⲢⲈⲦⲈⲚⲬⲰⲔ Ⲉ̇ⲂⲞⲖ Ⲉ̇ⲬⲰⲨ Ⲛ̇ⲚⲒⲀ̇ⲚⲀⲄᷘ

ⲤⲒⲤ ·ⲉ· ⲚⲈⲘ ϮⲬⲒⲚⲪⲰⲨ ⲌⲒⲦⲈⲚ ⲚⲒⲤⲚⲎⲞⲨ

Ⲛ̇Ⲉ̇ⲠⲒⲤⲔⲞⲠⲞⲤ ⲈⲐⲚⲎⲞⲨ ⲨⲀⲢⲰⲦⲈⲚ ⲚⲈⲘⲀⲨ

120 ⲔⲀⲦⲀϮⲔⲀⲌⲤ ⲈⲦⲬⲎ Ⲉ̇ⳝⲢⲎⲒ ·ⲉ· ⲞⲨⲞⲌ Ⲉ̇Ϯ ⲚⲀⲨ

ⲚⲚⲎ ⲈⲦⲈⲚⲞⲨϤ ⲚⲆⲒⲔⲈⲰⲘⲀ ·Ⲉ· ⲚⲈⲘ ⲚⲈϤ

ⲠⲀⲢⲀⲆⲞⲤⲒⲤ ·Ⲉ· ⲞⲨⲞⲌ ⲚⲀⲒϤ ⲚⲀⲠⲢⲰⲞⲨϤ

ⲌⲒⲚⲀ ⲚⲐⲞϤ ⲌⲰϤ ⲚⲦⲈϤϢⲰⲠⲒ ⲈϤⲤⲢⲰϤⲦ

ⲈⲦⲰⲂⲌ ·Ⲉ· ⲚⲈⲘ ⲈⲈⲢⲠⲢⲈⲤⲂⲈⲨⲒⲚ ⲈⲌⲢⲎⲒ

125 ⲈⲬⲰⲞⲨ ⲘⲠⲒⲈⲌⲞⲞⲨ ⲚⲈⲘ ⲠⲒⲈⲬⲰⲢⲌ ·Ⲉ· ⲚⲈⲘ

ⲈⲦⲤⲂⲰ ⲚⲰⲞⲨ ⲈⲐⲂⲈⲠⲞⲨⲬⲀⲒ ⲚⲚⲞⲨⲮⲨⲬⲎ ·Ⲉ·

ⲈⲐⲂⲈ ⲬⲈ ⲠⲒⲈⲨⲀⲄⲄⲈⲖⲒⲞⲚ ⲈⲐⲞⲨⲀⲂ ⲬⲰ Ⲙ

ⲘⲞⲤ ⲬⲈ ⲠⲒⲈⲢⲄⲀⲦⲎⲤ ϤⲈⲘⲠϢⲀ ⲚⲦⲈϤⲂⲈⲔⲈ

ϤⲬⲰ ⲘⲘⲞⲤ ⲚⲬⲈ ⲪⲖⲀⲤ ⲘⲠⲒⲤⲐⲞⲒⲚⲞⲨϤⲒ

130 ⲠⲀⲨⲖⲞⲤ ·Ⲉ·

ⲬⲈ ⲚⲒⲘ ⲈⲐⲚⲀⲀⲘⲞⲚⲒ ⲚⲞⲨⲞⲌⲒ ⲚⲈⲤⲰⲞⲨ ⲞⲨⲞⲌ

ⲚⲦⲈϤϢⲦⲈⲘⲞⲨⲰⲘ ⲈⲂⲞⲖ ϦⲈⲚⲠⲈϤⲈⲢⲰⲦ

ⲒⲈ ⲚⲒⲘ ⲈϤⲀⲨϬⲞ ⲚⲞⲨⲒⲀⲌⲀⲖⲞⲖⲒ ⲞⲨⲞⲌ ⲚⲦⲈϤ

ϢⲦⲈⲘⲞⲨⲰⲘ ⲈⲂⲞⲖ ϦⲈⲚⲠⲈϤⲞⲨⲦⲀⲌ ·Ⲉ·

135 ⲞⲨⲞⲌ ⲒⲤⲬⲈ ⲀⲚⲤⲒⲦ ⲚⲰⲦⲈⲚ ⲚⲌⲀⲚⲠⲚⲀⲦⲒⲔⲞⲨ

ⲞⲨⲌⲰⲞⲨ ⲠⲈ ⲬⲈ ⲚⲦⲈⲚⲰⲤϦ ⲚⲚⲈⲦⲈⲚⲤⲀⲢⲔⲒⲔⲞⲚ

ⲠϬⲤ ⲄⲀⲢ ⲀϤⲀⲨⲐⲀⲌⲘⲈϤ ⲚⲞⲨⲞⲨⲎⲂ ⲈⲬⲰⲞⲨ

ⲘⲪⲢⲎϮ ⲈⲦⲈϤ ⲬⲰ ⲘⲘⲞⲤ ⲚⲬⲈ ⲠⲒⲀⲠⲞⲤⲦⲞⲖⲞⲤ ⲋ

ⲞⲨⲞⲌ ⲘⲠⲀⲢⲈⲞⲨⲀⲒ ϬⲒ ⲚⲀϤ ⲘⲠⲒⲦⲀⲒⲞ ⲘⲘⲀⲨ   (Red)

140 ⲀⲦϤ ⲀⲖⲖⲀ ⲀϤⲐⲰⲌⲈⲘ ⲘⲘⲞϤ ⲚⲬⲈ ⲪϮ   (Red)

ⲘⲪⲢⲎϮ ⲚⲀⲀⲢⲰⲚ ·Ⲉ·

ⲆⲀⲨⲒⲆ ⲠⲒⲈⲢⲞⲮⲀⲖⲦⲎⲤ ⲬⲰ ⲘⲘⲞⲤ ·Ⲉ· ⲬⲈ ⲚⲐⲞⲔ

ⲠⲈ ⲪⲞⲨⲎⲂ ϢⲀⲈⲚⲈⲌ ⲔⲀⲦⲀⲦⲦⲀⲜⲒⲤ ⲘⲘⲈⲖ

ⲬⲒⲤⲈⲆⲈⲔ ·Ⲉ· ⲈⲚⲬⲰ ⲆⲈ ⲚⲚⲀⲒ ⲚⲰⲦⲈⲚ

145 ⲀⲚ ⲌⲰⲤ ⲬⲈ ⲈⲚⲘⲈⲨⲒ ⲈⲢⲰⲦⲈⲚ ⲬⲈ ⲈⲢⲈⲦⲈⲚ

ⲬⲞⲢⲌ ⲘⲈ ⲄⲈⲚⲈⲦⲰ ·Ⲉ· ⲀⲖⲖⲀ ⲈⲚⲤⲰⲞⲨⲚ ⲬⲈ

ⲈⲢⲈⲦⲈⲚⲘⲈⲌ ⲈⲂⲞⲖ ϦⲈⲚⲌⲘⲞⲦ ⲚⲒⲂⲈⲚ Ⲙ

ⲠⲚⲀⲦⲒⲔⲞⲚ ·Ⲉ· ⲈⲞⲨⲀⲌⲤⲀⲌⲚⲒ ⲆⲈ ⲚⲀⲚ ⲈϮ Ⲙ

ⲪⲘⲈⲨⲒ ⲚⲰⲦⲈⲚ ⲚⲈⲘ ⲈϮⲤⲂⲰ ·Ⲉ· ⲚⲈⲘ ⲈⲈⲢ

150 ⲚⲨⲪⲒⲚ ⲘⲘⲰⲦⲈⲚ ⲈⲪⲘⲎⲚ ·Ⲉ·

Ⲫ︦ϯ Ⲇⲉ ⲡⲓⲗⲟⲅⲟⲥ ⲉϥⲑⲣⲉⲡⲉⲩϫⲓⲛⲓ ⲛⲉⲙ ⲡⲉϥ

ϫⲓⲛⲫⲟϩ ϣⲁⲣⲱⲧⲉⲛ ·ⲉ· ϣⲱⲡⲓ ⲛⲱⲧⲉⲛ

ⲛ̀ⲟⲩⲥⲙⲟⲩ ·ⲉ· ⲉⲝⲉⲛⲛⲉⲧⲉⲛϯⲙⲓ ⲛⲉⲙ ⲛⲉⲧⲉⲛ

ⲭⲱⲣⲁ ·ⲉ· ⲟⲩⲟϩ ⲛ̀ⲧⲉⲧⲉϥϩⲓⲣⲏⲛⲏ ⲛⲉⲙ ⲡⲉϥ

155   ⲥⲉⲙⲛⲓ ⲙⲏⲛ ⲉ̀ⲃⲟⲗ ϧⲉⲛⲧⲉϥⲉⲕⲕⲗⲏⲥⲓⲁ̀ ·ⲉ·

ⲛⲉⲙ ϯⲟⲓⲕⲟⲩⲙⲉⲛⲏ ⲧⲏⲣⲥ ·ⲉ· ⲟⲩⲟϩ ⲛ̀ⲧⲉϥⲛⲟ

ϩⲉⲙ ⲛ̀ⲛⲉⲛⲯⲩⲭⲏ ·ⲉ· ⲉⲑⲣⲉⲛⲓ̀ⲛⲓ ⲛⲁϥ ⲉ̀ⲡϣⲱⲓ

ⲙ̀ⲡⲓⲱ̀ⲟⲩ ⲛⲉⲙ ⲡⲓⲧⲁⲓⲟ̀ ·ⲉ· ⲛⲉⲙ ϯⲡⲣⲟⲥⲕⲩⲛⲏⲥⲓⲥ

ⲛⲉⲙ ⲡⲉϥⲓⲱⲧ ⲛ̀ⲁ̀ⲅⲁⲑⲟⲥ ·ⲉ· ⲛⲉⲙ ⲡⲓⲡ̅ⲛ̅ⲁ̅ ⲉⲑ̅ⲩ̅ⲁⲃ

160   ⲛ̀ⲣⲉϥⲧⲁⲛϧⲟⲟⲩ ⲟⲩⲟϩ ⲛ̀ⲟ̀ⲙⲟⲟⲩⲥⲓⲟⲥ ⲛⲉⲙⲁϥ ·ⲉ·

ϯⲛⲟⲩ ⲛⲉⲙ ⲛ̀ⲥⲏⲟⲩ ⲛⲓⲃⲉⲛ ·ⲉ· ⲛⲉⲙ ϣⲁⲉ̀ⲛⲉϩ

ⲛ̀ⲧⲉ ⲛⲓⲉ̀ⲛⲉϩ ⲧⲏⲣⲟⲩ ⲁ̀ⲙⲏⲛ

✝ϩⲓⲣⲏⲛⲏ ⲛ̀ⲧⲉ ⲡ̅ϭ̅ⲥ̅ ⲉⲧⲁⲥⲉⲙⲧⲟⲛ ⲙ̀ⲙⲟⲥ ⲉ̀ϫⲉⲛ

ⲛⲉϥⲙⲁⲑⲏⲧⲏⲥ ⲉⲑⲟⲩⲁⲃ ·ⲉ· ⲛⲉⲙ ⲛⲉϥⲥⲱⲧⲡ ⲛ̀

165   ⲁ̀ⲅⲓⲟⲥ ⲉⲥⲉ̀ⲙⲧⲟⲛ ⲙ̀ⲙⲟⲥ ⲉ̀ϩⲣⲏⲓ ⲉ̀ϫⲱϥ

ⲛⲉⲙⲱⲧⲉⲛ ·ⲉ· ⲛⲉⲙ ⲡⲉϥϩⲙⲟⲧ ⲛⲉⲙ ⲡⲉϥ

ⲥⲙⲟⲩ ·ⲉ· ⲁ̀ⲙⲏⲛ ·ⲉ·

⳨ ———— ‿‿‿ ‿‿‿ ‿‿‿ ———— ⳨

Ⲧⲁⲓ ⲉ̀ⲡⲓⲥⲧⲟⲗⲏ ⲛ̀ⲥⲩⲥⲧⲁⲧⲓⲕⲏ ⲛ̀ⲧⲉⲡⲉⲛⲓⲱⲧ

ⲁⲃⲃⲁ ⲧⲓⲙⲟⲑⲉⲟⲥ ⲡⲉⲧⲉⲛⲉ̀ⲡⲓⲥⲕⲟⲡⲟⲥ ·ⲉ· ⲁⲛ

170   ⲧⲁⲭⲣⲟⲥ ϧⲉⲛⲛⲉⲛϫⲓϫ ⲙ̀ⲙⲓⲛ ⲙ̀ⲙⲟⲛ ·ⲉ·

ⲁⲛⲟⲩⲟ̀ⲣⲡⲥ ⲇⲉ ⲛⲉⲙ ⲛⲓⲉ̀ⲡⲓⲥⲕⲟⲡⲟⲥ ⲛ̀ⲟ̀ⲥⲓⲟ̅ⲧ̅ⲁ

ⲧⲁⲧⲟⲥ ⲉⲑⲛⲏⲟⲩ ϣⲁⲣⲱⲧⲉⲛ ⲛⲉⲙⲁⲩ ·ⲉ·
sic

ⲉⲑⲣⲟⲩⲓ̀ⲛⲓ ⲙ̀ⲡⲉϥⲑⲣⲟⲛⲓⲥⲙⲟⲥ ·ⲉ· ϧⲉⲛ ⲧⲉⲕ

ⲕⲗⲏⲥⲓⲁ̀ ⲛ̀ⲧⲉ ⲛⲓⲉ̀ⲡⲓⲥⲕⲟⲡⲟⲥ ⲛ̀ⲧⲉ ⲡⲓⲑⲱϣ

175   ⲛ̀ϧⲏ̅ⲧ̅ⲥ̅ ·ⲉ· ⲉ̀ⲟⲩⲱ̀ⲟⲩ ⲙ̀ⲡ̅ϭ̅ⲥ̅ ϣⲁⲉ̀ⲛⲉϩ ⲁⲙⲏⲛ ·ⲉ·

⳨ ———— ·· ———— ————— ⳨

A.

	ϧⲉⲛⲫⲣⲁⲛ ⲛ̀ⲧⲧⲣⲓⲁⲥ ⲉ̀ⲑⲟⲩⲁⲃ
	ⲫⲓⲱⲧ ⲛⲉⲙ ⲡϣⲏⲣⲓ ⲛ̅ⲉ̅ⲙ̅ ⲡⲓⲡⲛ̅ⲁ̅ ⲉⲑⲩ̅
	ϥⲣⲁⲟⲩⲱ̀ ⲛ̀ϫⲉ ⲡⲓϩⲏⲕⲓ ϧⲉⲛ
	ⲛⲓϣⲏⲣⲓ ⲛ̀ⲧⲉⲛⲓⲣⲱⲙⲓ ⲉⲑⲃⲉ
5. 180	ⲡⲁⲩϫⲁⲓ ⲛ̀ⲧⲉⲛⲉⲩⲛⲟⲃⲓ ⲙⲓⲭⲁⲏⲗ
	ⲛ̀ⲧⲉⲡⲓⲑⲣⲟⲛⲟⲥ ⲛ̀ⲧⲉⲑⲣⲉⲃⲓ ⲛ̅ⲉ̅ⲙ̅
	ⲛⲏ ⲉⲧⲛⲉⲙⲁϥ ⲛ̀ⲧⲭⲓⲣⲱⲧⲟⲛⲓⲁ
	ⲛ̀ⲧⲉⲡⲉⲛⲓⲱⲧ ⲉⲧⲧⲁⲓⲏⲟⲩⲧ ⲟⲩⲟϩ
	ⲛ̀ϩⲟⲩⲧⲁⲓⲟⲩ ⲡⲓⲡⲣⲉⲥⲃⲩⲧⲉⲣⲟⲥ
10. 185	ⲧⲓⲙⲟⲑⲉⲟⲥ ⲡⲓⲗⲩⲃⲓ ϧⲉⲛⲡⲉϥ
	ⲅⲉⲛⲟⲥ ⲛ̀ⲏⲅⲟⲩⲙⲉⲛⲟⲥ ⲛⲉⲙ ⲧⲉϥ
	ⲙⲉⲧⲉⲡⲓⲥⲕⲟⲡⲟⲥ ϧⲉⲛⲡⲉϫⲟⲟⲩ
	ⲛ̀ⲧⲕⲩⲣⲓⲁⲕⲏ ⲛ̀ⲥⲟⲩ ⲓ̅ⲑ̅ ⲙ̀ⲡⲓⲁⲃⲟⲧ
	ⲁⲑⲱⲣ ✠ ⲁ̅ⲡ̅ⲏ̅ ϧⲉⲛ ⲧ̀ⲁⲅⲓⲁ
15. 190	ⲛ̀ⲕⲁⲑⲟⲗⲓⲕⲏ ⲛ̀ⲉⲕⲕⲗⲏⲥⲓⲁ ⲛ̀ⲧⲉ
	ⲧ̀ⲁⲅⲓⲁ ⲙⲁⲣⲓⲁ ⲧ̀ⲁⲛⲁⲃⲁⲑⲏ ⲉⲧϧⲉ̅
	ⲡⲓⲫⲱⲥⲧⲁⲧⲟⲛ ⲛ̀ⲧⲉⲭⲏⲙⲓ
	Ⲉ̀ⲃⲟⲗ ϧⲉⲛⲧⲭⲓϫ ⲙ̀ⲡⲉⲛⲓⲱ̅ⲧ̅ ⲉⲧ
	ⲧⲁⲓⲏⲟⲩⲧ ⲕⲁⲧⲁ ⲁ̀ⲣⲉⲧⲏ ⲛⲓⲃⲉⲛ
20 195	ⲡⲓⲛⲓϣϯ ϧⲉⲛⲛⲓⲡⲁⲧⲣⲓⲁⲣⲭⲏⲥ
	ⲁⲃⲃⲁ ⲅⲁⲃⲣⲓⲏⲗ ⲡⲓⲡⲁⲧⲣⲓⲁⲣⲭⲏ̅
	ⲉ̀ϫⲉⲛⲡⲓⲑⲣⲟⲛⲟⲥ ⲙ̀ⲙⲁⲣⲕⲟⲥ ⲡⲓⲁ̀ⲡⲟ̅
	ⲧⲟⲗⲟⲥ ⲡⲓ̀ⲑⲣⲟⲛⲟⲥ ⲛ̀ⲧⲉⲧⲡⲟⲗⲓⲥ
	ⲙ̀ⲙⲁⲓⲛⲟⲩϯ ⲣⲁⲕⲟϯ ⲛⲉⲙ ⲧⲭⲱⲣⲁ ⲧⲏⲣ̅
25. 200	ⲛ̀ⲭⲏⲙⲓ ⲛⲉⲙ ⲡⲕⲁϩⲓ ⲛ̀ⲛⲓⲉ̀ⲑⲁⲩϣ
	ⲛⲉⲙ ⲧⲗⲩⲃⲓ ⲛⲉⲙ ϯⲉ̅ⲙ̅ⲃⲁⲕⲓ ⲉⲧϧⲉ̅
	ⲡⲉⲙⲉⲛⲧ ⲛⲉⲙ ⲛⲟⲩⲑⲱϣ ⲧⲏⲣⲟⲩ
	ⲁ̅ϥⲫⲱϣⲉⲛ ⲙ̀ⲡⲁⲓⲡⲣⲉⲥⲃⲩⲧⲉⲣⲟ̅
	ⲛ̀ⲏⲅⲟⲩⲙⲉⲛⲟⲥ ⲛⲉⲙ ⲉ̀ⲡⲓⲥⲕⲟⲡⲟ̅
30. 205	ⲟⲩⲟϩ ⲁϥϯⲣⲁⲛ ⲉ̀ⲣⲟϥ ⲭⲉ ⲧⲓⲙⲟⲑⲉ̅ⲟ̅ⲥ̅

B.

ϧⲉⲛⲫⲣⲁⲛ ⲙ̀ⲫⲓⲱⲧ ⲛⲉⲙ ⲡϣⲏⲣⲓ
ⲛⲉⲙ ⲡⲓⲡⲛ̅ⲁ̅ ⲉ̅ⲑ̅
ϥⲉⲣⲟⲩⲱ̀ ⲛ̀ϫⲉ ⲡⲓϩⲏⲕⲓ ϧⲉⲛⲛⲓϣⲏⲣⲓ
ⲛ̀ⲧⲉⲛⲓⲣⲱⲙⲓ ⲛ̀ⲧⲉⲛⲉⲩⲛⲟⲃⲓ ⲡⲉⲧⲣⲟⲥ
ⲡⲓⲉⲡⲓⲥⲕⲟⲡⲟⲥ ⲛ̀ⲧⲉⲧⲡⲟⲗⲓⲥ ⲙ̀ⲙⲁⲓⲡ̅ⲭ̅ⲥ̅
ϣⲙⲟⲩⲛ ⲃ̅ ⲧⲱⲛ ⲟⲛⲟⲙⲁ ⲁⲩⲧⲏⲥ
ⲛⲉⲙ ⲛⲏ ⲉⲑⲛⲉⲙⲁϥ ⲙ̀ⲡⲓⲭⲓⲣⲱⲧⲓⲟ̅ⲥ̅ [ⲟⲛ]
ⲛ̀ⲧⲉⲡⲉⲛⲓⲱⲧ ⲉⲧⲧⲁⲓⲏⲟⲩⲧ ⲙ̀ⲡⲣⲉⲥⲃⲩ
ⲧⲉⲣⲟⲥ ⲧⲓⲙⲟⲑⲉⲟⲥ ⲡⲓⲗⲩⲃⲓ ϧⲉⲛⲡⲉϥ
ⲅⲉⲛⲟⲥ ⲛⲉⲙ ⲧⲉϥⲙⲉⲧⲉ̀ⲡⲓⲥⲕⲟⲡⲟⲥ
ϧⲉⲛⲡⲉϫⲟⲟⲩ ⲛ̀ⲧⲉⲧⲕⲩⲣⲓⲁⲕⲏ ⲛ̀ⲥⲟⲩ ⲓ̅ⲑ̅
ⲙ̀ⲡⲓⲁ̀ⲃⲟⲧ ⲁ̀ⲑⲱⲣ ✠ ⲁ̅ⲡ̅ⲏ̅
ϧⲉⲛ ⲧ̀ⲁⲅⲓⲁ ⲛ̀ⲕⲁⲑⲟⲗⲓⲕⲏ ⲛ̀ⲁⲡⲟⲥⲧⲟ̅
ⲗⲓⲕⲏ ⲛ̀ⲉⲕⲕⲗⲏⲥⲓⲁ ⲛ̀ⲧⲉ ⲧ̀ⲁⲅⲓⲁ ⲙⲁⲣⲓⲁ
ⲧ̀ⲁⲛⲁⲃⲁⲑⲏ ⲉⲧϧⲉⲛ ⲡⲓⲫⲱⲥ̅ⲧ̅ⲁⲧⲟⲛ
ⲛ̀ⲧⲉⲭⲏⲙⲓ
Ⲉ̀ⲃⲟⲗ ϧⲉⲛⲧⲭⲓϫ ⲙ̀ⲡⲉⲛⲓⲱ̅ⲧ̅ ⲉ̀ⲧⲁⲓⲏⲟⲩ̅ⲧ̅
ⲡⲓⲛⲓϣϯ ϧⲉⲛⲛⲓⲡⲁⲧⲣⲓⲁⲣⲭⲏⲥ ⲁⲃⲃⲁ
ⲅⲁⲃⲣⲓⲏⲗ ⲡⲓⲡⲁⲧ̅ⲣ̅ⲓⲁⲣⲭⲏⲥ ⲉϫⲉⲛ
ⲡⲓⲑⲣⲟⲛⲟⲥ ⲙ̀ⲙⲁⲣⲕⲟⲥ ⲡⲓⲁ̀ⲡⲟⲥⲧⲟⲗⲟⲥ
ⲡⲓⲑⲣⲟⲛⲟⲥ ⲛ̀ⲧⲉⲧⲡⲟⲗⲓⲥ ⲙ̀ⲙⲁⲓⲛⲟⲩϯ
ⲣⲁⲕⲟϯ ⲛⲉⲙ ⲧⲭⲱⲣⲁ ⲧⲏⲣⲥ ⲛ̅ⲧ̅ⲉⲭⲏⲙⲓ
ⲛⲉⲙ ⲡⲕⲁϩⲓ ⲛ̅ⲧ̅ⲉ ⲛⲓⲉ̀ⲑⲁⲩϣ ⲛⲉⲙ ϯⲃⲓ [sic]
ⲛⲉⲙ ϯⲉ̅ⲙ̅ⲃⲁⲕⲓ ⲉⲧϧⲉⲛⲧ̅ⲟ̅ⲙⲉⲛⲧ̅ [sic]
ⲛⲉⲙ ⲛⲟⲩⲑⲱϣ ⲧⲏⲣⲟⲩ
ⲁϥⲫⲱϣⲉⲛ ⲙ̀ⲡⲁⲓⲡⲣⲉⲥⲃⲩⲧⲉⲣⲟⲥ
ⲛ̀ϩ̅ⲅⲟⲩⲙⲉⲛⲟⲥ ⲛⲉⲙ ⲉⲡⲓⲥⲕⲟⲡⲟⲥ· [sic]
ⲟⲩⲟϩ ⲁϥϯⲣⲁⲛ ⲉⲣⲟϥ ⲭⲓ ⲧⲓⲙⲟⲑⲉⲟ̅ⲥ̅ [sic]
ⲕⲁⲧⲁⲡⲉϥⲣⲁⲛ ϧⲉⲛ ⲧⲙⲉⲧ̅ⲡ̅ⲣⲉⲥ
ⲃⲩⲧⲉⲣⲟⲥ ⲛ̀ϫⲉ ⲡⲉⲛⲓⲱ̅ⲧ̅ ⲉⲧ̅ⲧ̅ⲁ

ΚΑΤΑΠΕΥΡΑΝ ϨΕΝΤΜΕΤΠΡΕС
ΒΥΤΕΡΟС Ν̄ϪΕ ΠΕΝΙѠΤ ⲘΠΑΤ
ΡΙΑΡΧΗС ΕΤΑΝΕΡϢΟΡΠ Ⲛ̄ϪΕΠΕΙⲢΑϤ
ΕϪΕΝΠΙⲐΡΟΝΟС Ν̄ΑΠΑΧѠΡΟС

35   210   ΕΤϨΕΝΠΚΑϨΙ Ν̄ⲦⲖΥΒΙ ΦϮ
ΝΤΕΤϤΕ ΕϤΕΤΑϪΡΟ ⲘΠΕΝ
ΠΑΤΡΙΑΡΧΗС ΑΒΒΑ ΓΑΒΡΙΗⲖ ⲈϪⲈϤ
ΠΕϤⲐΡΟΝΟС Ν̄ϨΑⲘΜΗΥ Ν̄ΡΟⲘΠΙ
ΝΕⲘ ϨΑΝϹΗΟΥ Ν̄ϨΙΡΗΝΙΚΟϤ ⲀⲘΗⲚ

40   215   ΕϹⲈϢѠΠΙ ΕϹⲈϢѠΠΙ
ⲨϹϨΕΝΑΙϹⲦΥΧΟ̄ Ν̄ϪΕ ΠΙϨΗΚΙ
ⲘΙΧΑΗⲖ ϨΕΝϹΟΥ Κ̄Ϩ ⲘΠΙΑΒⲞⲦ
ⲀⲐѠΡ ϨΕΝ ⳨ΡΟⲘΠΙ ΕΤΑΝΕΡϢΟΡΠ
ⲀⲚϪΕΠΕϹΡΑΝ ΙϹ ⳨ⲘⲈⲦⲀⲚⲞⲒⲀ ΧѠ ΝΗΙ

45   220   ⲈΒⲞⲖ ☉ ϨΕΝΟΥϨΙΡΗΝΗ Ν̄ⲦⲈⲪ ⲀⲘΗⲚ

C.   β̄

ⲨΡΑⲞΥⲰ̄ ⲀⲚⲞⲔ ΠΙΕⲖⲀ̄ ⲘΑΡΚΟϹ ⲖⲒ
ⲦⲨ̄ΡⲄⲞ̄ ΤΟΥⲢⲐΡΟΝΟΥ ΤΗϹ ΠΟⲖΕΟϹ
ΚΕΒΤѠ ΝΕⲘ ΝΕϹⲐΟΥ ΚΕ ΔΙΑΤΟΧⲞ̄
ΤΟΥ ⳨ΡϹ ΗⲘѠΝ ΑΒΒΑ ΓΑΒΡΙΗⲖ

5   225   ⳨ΡΙΑΡΧⲨ̄ ΤΗϹ ⲘⲈΓΑⲖⲨ̄ ΠΟⲖΕѠϹ ⲀⲖⲈ
ϪⲀⲚⲆΡΙΑϹ ΚΕ ΤΗϹ ⲄⲈⲠⲦⲈѠϹ·ΚΕΡΙΑϹ
ΠΕΝΤΑΠΟⲖΕѠϹ ⲪⲢⲒ̈ΚⲒⲀϹ ΚΕ ⲚⲨ̄ΒΙΑϹ
ϨΟⲘΙΤΗϹ ΚΕ ⲐⲈⲞⲠⲒⲀϹ ΕΠⲒ ⲦⲨ̄ ⲐΡΟⲚⲨ̄
ΤΗϹ ΠΟⲖⲈѠ̈ ΑΡⲘⲞⲚ̄ ΝΕⲘ ΝΕϹⲐΟϢϤ

10   230   ΟΥΟϨ ΑΙΕΡϹΥⲘⲘⲘΕΤΟΧΙΝ ϨΕΝΠΙϪⲒ̈
ⲐΡΟΝΙϹⲘΟϹ ΝΕⲘ ΠΙΧΑϪΙΧ·ΕϪⲈⲚ
ΠΕⲚΙⲰ̄ ⲚⲞϹⲒⲞ̄ⲦΑⲦΟϹ ΚΕ ⲐΡⲒϹⲘⲀⲔⲀⲢⲒ
ΟϹ ΚΕ ΠΑΝΑΡΕΤΟϹ ΠΕΝΙⲰⲦ Ν̄ΕΠΙϹ
ΚΟΠΟϹ ΑΒΒΑ ΤΙⲘⲞⲐΕΟϹ ΠΙΕΠΙϹΚΟΠⲞ̄

15   235   ΝⲦⲈϮΠΟⲖΙϹ ⲘⲘⲀΙⳁⲭⲢϹ ⲀΠⲀΧѠΡⲀ̄

ΙΗⲞΥϮ ⲘΠΑΤΡΙΑΡΧΗϹ Ε̄ⲦⲀⲚΕΡ
ϢΟΡΠ ⲘΠΕϤⲢⲀⲚ ΕϪΕⲚΠΙⲐΡΟⲚΟϹ
ⲚⲀΠⲀΧѠⲢΟϹ ΕⲦϨΕⲚΠΚⲀϨΙ Ν̄Ⲧ
ⲖⲒΒⲨ̈ ΦϮ ⲚⲦΕϤⲪⲈ ΕϤΕⲦΑϪ
ⲢⲞ ⲘΠΕⲚΙⲰ̄ ΕⲦⲦⲀⲒ̈ΟΥϮ ⲘΠΑⲦ
ΡΙⲀⲢΧΗϹ ΑΒΒΑ ΓⲀΒΡΙΗⲖ Ⲛ̄ϨⲀϥ
ⲘΗⲨ Ν̄ΡΟⲘΠΙ ΝΕⲘ ϨⲀⲚϹΗΟΥ
Ν̄ϨΙΡΗⲚⲎⲔⲞⲚ ⲀⲘΗⲚ ⲈϹⲈϢѠΠΙ
ⲈϹⲈϢѠΠΙ

ⲨϹϨΕⲚΑΙϹⲦΥΧΟϹ Ν̄ϪⲈ ΠΙϨⲎ̄ΚⲒ
ΠΕⲦΡΟϹ ϨΕⲚϹΟΥ Κ̄Ϩ ⲘΠΙⲀΒⲞⲦ
ⲀⲐѠⲢ ϨΕⲚ ⳨ΡΟⲘΠΙ ΕⲦⲀⲚΕΡϢΟⲢⲠ̄
ⲘΠΕϹⲢⲀⲚ ΙϹ ⳨ⲘⲈⲦⲀⲚⲞⲒⲀ ΧѠ
ⲚΗⲒ ⲈΒⲞⲖ ϨΕⲚΟΥϨΙⲢΗⲚΗ ⲚⲦⲈ
ΦϮ ⲀⲘⲎⲚ

D.

✝ ⲞϤⲐⳤ ΕῩΔΙⲀⲖⲖⲞⲔⲦⲞⲚ ✝
ⳤΙⲈⲢⲀⲞΥⲰ̄ ⲀⲚⲞⲔ ΠΙΕⲖⲀ̄ ⲀⲐⲀⲚⲀϹΙΟϹ
ⲖⲒ̈ΤⲨⲢ ⲦⲨⲐⲢⲞⲚⲨ̈ ΤΗϹ ΠⲞⲖⲈⲞϹ
ΚѠϹⲂⲈⲢⲂⲒⲢ ΝⲈⲘ ⲚⲈϹⲐⲞⲨ
ΚⲈ ΔΙⲀⲦⲞⲬⲞϹ ⲦⲞⲨ ⳨ΡϹ ΗⲘⲰϤ
ⲀΒΒⲀ ⲄⲀΒⲢⲒⲎⲖ ⳨ΡⲒⲀⲢⲬⲨ̈ ⲦⲎϹ
ⲘⲈⲄⲀⲖⲞⲨ ⲠⲞⲖⲈⲰϹ ⲀⲖⲈϪⲀⲚⲆ
ⲢⲒⲀϹ ⲔⲈ ⲦⲎϹ ⲄⲈⲠⲦⲈⲰϹ Κ̄Ⲉ̄
ⲠⲈⲚⲦⲀⲠⲞⲖⲈⲰϹ· ⲪⲢⲒⲔⲒⲀ Κ̄Ⲉ̄
ⲚⲨ̈ΒⲒⲀϹ ϨⲞⲘⲒⲦⲎϹ ⲔⲈ ⲐⲈⲞⲠⲒⲀϹ̄
ⲈⲠⲒⲨ̈ ⲐⲢⲞⲚⲨ̈ ⲦⲎϹ ⲠⲞⲖⲈⲰ̈ ⲀⲢⲘⲞⲚ̄
ⲚⲈⲘ ⲚⲈϹⲐⲞⲨ ⲆⲞϨ ⲀⲒⲢϹⲨ̈
ⲘⲘⲈⲦⲞⲬⲒⲚ ϨⲈⲚⲠⲒϪⲒ̈ⲚⲐ
ⲢⲞⲚⲒϹⲘⲞϹ ⲚⲈⲘ ⲠⲒⲬⲀϪⲒⲬ
ⲈϪⲈⲚⲠⲈⲚⲒⲰⲦ ⲚⲞϹⲒⲞ̄ⲦⲀⲦⲞϹ

ⲚⲦⲈ†ⲖⲨⲂⲎ ⲚⲈⲘ ⲚⲈⲥⲐⲞⲨ ϨⲈⲚ†
ⲤⲨⲘⲘⲈⲦⲞⲬⲎ ⲘⲠⲈⲚⲒⲰⲦ ⲈⲐⲚⲞⲤⲒⲞ
ⲦⲀⲦⲞⲤ ⲔⲈ ⲐⲢⲒⲤⲘⲀⲔⲀⲢⲒⲞⲤ ⲀⲂⲂⲀ
ⲀⲐⲀⲚⲀⲤⲒⲀⲤ ⲠⲒⲈⲠⲒⲤⲔⲞⲠⲞⲤ ⲚⲦⲠⲞⲖ̅ⲓ̅ⲥ̅

20   240   ⲘⲘⲀⲒⲚⲞⲨ† ⲔⲞⲤⲂ̅Ⲃ̅Ⲉ̅Ⲣ̅ ⲚⲈⲘ ⲚⲈⲤⲐⲞⲨⲉ̅
ⲔⲈ ⲦⲠⲞⲖⲒⲤ ⲢⲘⲈⲚⲐ· ⲚⲈⲘ ⲚⲈⲤⲐⲞⲨ
ϨⲈⲚ ⲦⲀⲄⲒⲀ ⲚⲈⲔⲔⲖⲎⲤⲒⲀ ⲚⲦⲈⲠⲒ
ⲀⲄⲒⲞⲤ ⲘⲘⲀⲢⲦⲨⲢⲞⲤ ⲂⲒⲔⲦⲰⲢⲒⲞⲤ
ϨⲈⲚⲠⲒⲘⲞⲚⲀⲤⲦⲎⲢⲒⲞⲚ ⲚⲦⲈⲐ

25   245   ⲖⲀⲨⲢⲀ ϨⲈⲚⲠ̅ⲦⲰ̅ⲟ̅ ⲘⲠⲒⲰϢⲈ
ⲠⲒⲘⲈⲚ̅Ⲧ̅ Ⲛ̅ⲔⲀⲘⲞⲨⲖⲈ ϨⲈⲚⲠⲒⲂ̅
Ⲛ̅ⲔⲨⲢⲒⲀⲔⲎ Ⲉ̅Ⲑ̅ ⲚⲦⲚⲎⲤⲦⲀ[ⲥ] ⲘⲠⲒ
Ⲙ̅ ⲚⲈϨⲞ̅ⲟ̅ Ⲉ̅Ⲑ̅ ⲤⲞⲨ Ⲕ̅ ⲘⲠⲒⲀⲂⲟ̅Ⲧ̅
ⲘⲈⲬⲒⲢ †ⲢⲞⲘⲠⲒ Ⲗ̅ⲠⲎ Ⲛ̅ⲦⲈⲚⲒ

30   250   ⲀⲄⲒⲀⲤ ⲘⲘⲀⲢⲦⲨⲢⲞⲤ ⲈⲢⲈⲚϬⲤⲘ̅ⲟ̅
Ⲉ̅Ⲑ̅ ϢⲰⲠⲒ ⲚⲈⲘⲀⲚ ⲀⲘⲎⲚ ⲄⲈⲚⲒⲦⲞ
ⲈⲤⲈϢⲰⲠⲒ Ⲉ̅ⲞⲨⲰⲟ̅ Ⲙ̅Ⲫ̅†̅ ⲀⲘⲎⲚ†

35· — 300

ⲔⲈ ⲐⲢⲒⲤⲘⲀⲔⲀⲢⲒⲞⲤ ⲔⲈ ⲠⲀⲚⲀ
ⲢⲈⲦⲞⲤ ⲠⲈⲚⲒⲰⲦ ⲚⲈⲠⲒⲤⲔⲞⲠⲞⲥ
ⲀⲂⲂⲀ ⲦⲒⲘⲞⲐⲈⲞⲤ· ⲠⲒⲈⲠⲒⲤⲔ̅ⲟ̅ⲠⲞⲤ
Ⲛ̅ⲦⲈ ⲦⲠⲞⲖⲒⲤ ⲘⲘⲀ ⲒⲠⲬ̅Ⲣ̅ⲥ̅ ⲀⲠⲀ
ⲬⲰⲢⲀⲤ Ⲛ̅ⲦⲈ†ⲖⲨⲂⲎ ⲚⲈⲘ ⲚⲈⲉ̅
ⲐⲞⲨ· ϨⲈⲚ†ⲤⲨⲘⲘⲈⲦⲞⲬⲎ Ⲙ̅
ⲠⲈⲚⲒⲰ̅Ⲧ̅ ⲈⲐ ⲚⲞⲤⲒⲞⲦⲀⲦⲞⲤ ⲔⲈ [ⲐⲢⲒⲤ
ⲘⲀⲔⲀⲢⲒⲞⲤ· ⲀⲂⲂⲀ ⲘⲀⲢ[ⲔⲞⲤ
ⲠⲒⲈⲠⲒⲤⲔⲞⲠⲞⲤ Ⲛ̅ⲦⲠⲞⲖⲒⲤ ⲘⲘ[ⲀⲒ
Ⲛ̅Ⲟ̅Ⲩ̅†̅ ⲔⲈⲠⲦ̅ⲱ̅ ⲚⲈⲘ ⲚⲈⲤⲐⲞⲨ ⲔⲈ
ⲦⲠⲞⲖⲒⲤ ⲔⲈⲚⲀⲰⲢⲈ ᷍ⲚⲈⲘ ⲚⲈⲤⲐⲞⲨ
ϨⲈⲚ ⲦⲀⲄⲒⲀ ⲚⲈⲔⲔⲖⲎⲤⲒⲀ Ⲛ̅[ⲦⲈ
ⲠⲒⲀⲄⲒⲞⲤ ⲘⲘⲀⲢ[ⲦⲨ]ⲢⲞⲤ ⲂⲒⲔⲦⲰⲢ[ⲒⲞⲤ
ϨⲈⲚⲠⲒⲘⲞⲚⲀⲤⲦⲎⲢⲒⲞⲚ Ⲛ̅ⲦⲈⲐ
ⲖⲀⲨⲢⲀ ϨⲈⲚⲠ̅ⲦⲰ̅ⲟ̅ ⲘⲠⲒϢⲞⲨⲈ
ⲠⲒⲘⲈⲚ̅Ⲧ̅ Ⲛ̅ⲔⲀⲘⲞⲨⲖⲈ ϨⲈ[ⲚⲠⲒ
Ⲃ̅ Ⲛ̅ⲔⲨⲢⲒⲀⲔⲎ Ⲉ̅Ⲑ̅ Ⲛ̅[†ⲚⲎⲤⲦⲀⲤ Ⲙ
ⲠⲒⲘ̅ ⲚⲈϨⲞⲞⲨ Ⲉ̅Ⲑ̅ ⲤⲞⲨ Ⲕ̅ ⲘⲠⲒⲀ
Ⲃⲟ̅Ⲧ̅ ⲘⲈⲬⲒⲢ †ⲢⲞⲘⲠⲒ Ⲗ̅ⲠⲎ Ⲛ̅ⲦⲈ
ⲚⲒⲀⲄⲒⲞⲤ ⲘⲘⲀⲢⲦⲨⲢⲞⲤ ⲈⲢⲈ[Ⲛ̅]ϭ̅
ⲤⲘⲞⲨ Ⲉ̅Ⲑ̅ ϢⲰⲠⲒ ⲚⲈⲘ[ⲀⲚ ⲀⲘⲎⲚ
ⲄⲈⲚⲒⲦⲞ ⲈⲤⲈϢⲰⲠⲒ Ⲉ̅ⲞⲨⲰⲟ̅
Ⲙ̅Ⲫ̅†̅ ⲀⲘⲎⲚ†

Collation of Coptic Scroll of Bishop Timotheos with Paris MS. Arab. 203 (Bibliothèque Nationale)

	Timotheos		Paris
line			
1	ⲧⲟⲓⲥ ⲧⲁⲡⲁⲛⲧⲁ ⲧⲟⲩ ⲑⲉⲟⲩ ⲫⲓⲗⲟⲭⲣⲩⲧⲁⲧⲱ	fol. 166a	ⲧⲟⲓⲥ ⲧⲁⲡⲁⲛⲧⲏⲥ ⲧⲱ ⲟ̄ⲩ̄ ⲫⲓⲗⲟⲭⲣⲩⲧⲁⲧⲱ
3	ⲩⲡⲟⲇⲓⲁⲕⲟⲛⲟⲩ		omit
5	ⲧⲁⲁ̄ⲗⲱ ⲧⲏⲥ ⲡⲟⲗⲓⲥ		ⲧⲁ ⲗⲁⲱ̄ ⲧⲏ ⲡⲟⲗⲉⲟ̄ⲥ
8	ⲁⲃⲃⲁ ⲅⲁⲃⲣⲓⲏⲗ ⲡⲕ̄ⲩ̄ ⲡⲁⲧⲏⲣ ⲭⲉⲣⲉⲓⲛ		ⲡⲁⲡⲁ ⲡⲓⲙ ⲡⲕ̄ⲱ̄ ⲭⲁⲓⲣⲉⲓⲛ
12			omit
13			omit
16	ⲡⲟⲗⲓⲥ ⲣⲁⲕⲟϯ ⲛⲉⲙ ⲃⲁⲃⲩⲗⲱⲛ ⲛⲉⲙ ⲡⲉⲥⲑⲱϣ ⲛⲉⲙ ϯⲗⲩⲃⲏ ⲛⲉⲙ ⲡⲓⲉⲑⲁⲩϣ ⲛⲉⲙ ⲡⲏ ⲉⲧⲉ ⲡⲟⲩⲟⲩ ⲛⲉⲙ ⲉ̄ ⲙⲃⲁⲕⲓ ⲉⲧⲥⲁⲉⲛⲡⲉⲙⲉⲛⲧ ⲛⲉⲙ ⲫⲣⲓⲕⲓⲁ	fol. 166b	ⲡⲟⲗⲓⲥ ⲁⲗⲉⲍⲁⲛⲇⲣⲓⲁ ⲛⲉⲙ ⲃⲁⲃⲩⲗⲱⲛ ⲛⲉⲙ ⲡⲉⲥⲑⲱϣ ⲛⲉⲙ ϯⲗⲩⲃⲏ ⲛⲉⲙ ⲡⲓⲉⲑⲁⲩϣ ⲛⲉⲙ ⲡⲏ ⲉⲧⲉ ⲡⲟⲩⲟⲩ
21	ⲧⲉⲛⲧⲁⲙⲟ ⲧⲉ		ⲧⲉⲛⲧⲁⲙⲟ ⲇⲉ
27	ⲡ̄ⲧⲡⲟⲗⲓⲥ ⲙⲙⲁⲓⲭ̄ⲣ̄ⲥ̄ ⲡⲭⲱⲣⲁⲥ ⲛⲉⲙ ϯⲗⲩⲃⲏ ⲛⲉⲙ ⲡⲉⲥⲑⲱϣ ⲧⲏⲣⲟⲩ		ⲡⲡ̄ⲧⲡⲟⲗⲱⲥ ⲙⲙⲁⲓⲭ̄ⲣ̄ⲥ̄ ⲥⲁⲑⲟⲩ ⲛⲉⲙ ϯϣⲁⲓⲣⲓ
35	ⲛⲉⲙ ⲡⲟⲩⲭⲱⲣⲟⲥ	fol. 167a	ⲛⲉⲙ ⲡⲟⲩⲭⲱⲣⲓⲥⲕⲟⲥ
			sic
41	ⲥⲁⲉⲛⲟⲩⲁⲅⲁⲡⲏ		ⲥⲁⲉⲧⲉϥⲁⲅⲁⲡⲏ
60	ⲡⲓⲡⲣⲉⲥⲃⲩⲧⲉⲣⲟⲥ ⲫⲁⲡⲓⲃⲓⲟⲥ ⲛϣⲟⲩⲉ ⲡⲉ ⲡⲟⲩ ⲙⲙⲟϥ ⲧⲓⲙⲟⲑⲉⲟⲥ ⲕⲁⲧⲁ ⲫⲏ ⲉⲧⲉϥⲫⲱϣ ⲡⲣⲁⲡϯ. ϥⲁⲓ ⲁϥϣⲱⲡⲓ ⲛⲟⲩⲡⲣⲉⲥⲃⲩⲧⲉⲣⲟⲥ ⲟⲩⲟϩ ⲙⲙⲟ ⲡⲁⲭⲟⲥ ⲉⲭⲉⲛⲧⲉⲕⲕⲗⲏⲥⲓⲁ ⲛⲧⲉϯⲑⲉⲟⲧⲟⲕⲟⲥᶜ ⲉⲑⲟⲩⲁⲃ ϯⲁⲅⲓⲁ ⲙⲁⲣⲓⲁ ⲡⲭⲱⲣⲁⲥ ⲛⲉⲙ ϯⲗⲩⲃⲏ	fol. 168a	ⲡⲣⲉⲥⲃⲩⲧⲉⲣⲟⲥ ⲉⲭⲉⲛⲡⲓⲙⲟⲛⲁⲥⲧⲏⲣⲓⲟⲛ ⲛⲧⲉⲡⲓⲛⲓϣϯ ⲛⲓⲙ ⲡⲓⲙⲟⲛⲁⲭⲟⲥ ⲛⲧⲉⲗⲓⲟⲥ ⲫⲁⲡⲓⲃⲓⲟⲥ ⲛϣⲟⲩⲉ ⲡⲉⲩⲛⲟⲩ ⲙⲙⲟϥ ⲛⲓⲙ ⲡⲓⲡⲣⲟⲉⲥⲧⲟⲥ ⲛⲧⲉⲡⲓⲙⲟⲛⲁⲥⲧⲏⲣⲓⲟⲛ ⲉⲑ̄ⲟ̄ ⲛⲧⲉⲡⲓⲁⲅⲓⲟⲥ ⲛⲓⲙ ⲛⲧⲉⲡⲧⲱⲟⲩ ⲛϣⲟⲣⲏⲧ ⲛⲉⲙ ⲡⲓⲙⲟⲛⲁⲥⲧⲏⲣⲓⲟⲛ ⲛⲧⲉⲡⲓⲁⲛⲁⲃⲁⲭⲱⲛⲓ ⲥⲁⲉⲛⲡⲉⲑⲱϣ ⲛⲣⲁⲕⲱϯ
66	sic ⲟⲩⲟϩ ⲛ̄ⲁⲓϥ ⲡⲅ̄ⲧⲟⲙⲉⲛⲟⲥ		ⲟⲩⲟϩ ⲁⲡⲁⲓϥ ⲡⲅ̄ⲧⲟⲙⲉⲛⲟⲥ
73	ⲥⲁⲉⲛⲡⲓⲫⲱⲥⲧⲁⲧⲟⲛ ⲛⲧⲉⲭⲏⲙⲓ ⲑⲏ ⲉⲧⲣⲱⲓⲥ	fol. 168b	ⲥⲁⲉⲛⲡⲓⲫⲱⲥⲧⲁⲧⲟⲛ ⲛⲧⲉϯⲛⲓϣϯ ⲛⲃⲁⲕⲓ ⲃⲁⲃⲩⲗⲱⲛ
122	ⲟⲩⲟϩ ⲛ̄ⲁⲓϥ ⲛⲁⲧⲣⲱⲟⲩϣ	fol. 170b	ⲟⲩⲟϩ ⲉⲭⲓϥ ⲛⲁⲧⲣⲱⲟⲩϣ
135	ⲟⲩⲟϩ ⲭⲉ ⲓⲥⲭⲉ ⲁⲛⲥⲓϯ	fol. 171a	ⲟⲩⲟϩ ⲟⲛ ⲭⲉ ⲓⲥⲭⲉ ⲁⲛⲥⲓϯ
160	ⲛⲣⲉϥⲧⲁⲛⲥⲟⲟⲩ	fol. 172a	ⲛⲣⲉϥⲧⲁⲛⲥⲟ
168	ⲧⲁⲓ ⲉ̀ⲡⲓⲥⲧⲟⲗⲏ ⲛⲥⲩⲥⲧⲁⲧⲓⲕⲏ ⲛⲧⲉⲡⲉⲛⲓⲱⲧ ⲁⲃⲃⲁ ⲧⲓⲙⲟⲑⲉⲟⲥ ⲡⲉⲧⲉⲛⲉ̀ⲡⲓⲥⲕⲟⲡⲟⲥ	fol. 172b	ⲧⲁⲓ ⲉⲡⲓⲥⲧⲟⲗⲏ ⲛⲥⲓⲥⲧⲁⲇⲓⲕⲏ ⲛⲧⲉⲁⲃⲃⲁ ⲛⲓⲙ ⲡⲓⲉⲡⲓⲥⲕⲟⲡⲟⲥ ⲛⲧⲱⲧⲉⲛ
171	ⲁⲡⲟⲩⲟⲣⲡⲥ ⲇⲉ ⲛⲉⲙ ⲡⲓⲉⲡⲓⲥⲕⲟⲡⲟⲥ ⲛⲟ̀ⲥⲓⲟ̀ⲧⲁ sic ⲧⲁⲧⲟⲥ ⲉⲑⲛⲟⲩ ϣⲁⲣⲱⲧⲉⲛ ⲛⲉⲙⲁϥϯ. ⲉⲑⲣⲟⲩⲅⲓⲛⲓⲙⲓⲙⲡⲉϥⲑⲣⲟⲡⲓⲥⲙⲟⲥ. ⲥⲁⲉⲛⲧⲉⲕ ⲕⲗⲏⲥⲓⲁ̀ ⲛⲧⲉⲡⲓⲉⲡⲓⲥⲕⲟⲡⲟⲥ ⲛⲧⲉⲡⲓⲑⲱϣ ⲛⲥ̀ⲛⲧⲥ·ⲉ̀ⲟⲩⲱ̀ⲟⲩ ⲙⲡ̄ⲥ̄ ϣⲁⲉⲛⲉϩ ⲁⲙⲏⲛ·ϯ.		ⲁⲡⲟⲩⲱⲣⲡ ⲇⲉ ϣⲁⲡⲓⲉⲡⲓⲥⲕⲟⲡⲟⲥ ⲛⲟⲥⲓⲟⲧⲁⲧⲟⲥ ⲉⲑⲣⲟⲩⲓⲣⲓ ⲙⲡⲉϥⲑⲣⲟⲡⲓⲥⲙⲟⲥ ⲥⲁⲉⲛⲧⲉⲕⲕⲗⲏⲥⲓⲁ ⲉⲧⲩⲓⲣⲓ ⲙ̀ⲡⲉⲑⲣⲟⲡⲓⲥⲙⲟⲥ ⲛⲧⲉⲡⲓⲉⲡⲓⲥⲕⲟⲡⲟⲥ sic ϣ ⲛⲧⲉⲡⲓⲉⲡⲓⲱ̄ ⲛⲥ̀ⲛⲧⲉ ⲉ̀ⲟⲩⲱⲟⲩⲡ̄ⲥ̄ ϣⲁⲉⲛⲉϩ ⲁⲙⲏⲛ

Translation of the Coptic Text

* indicates a note on pp. 22 ff.

IN THE NAME OF THE FATHER AND THE SON
AND THE HOLY SPIRIT, ONE GOD

TO ALL GOD'S MOST CHRIST-LOVING PRIESTS, DEACONS, SUBDEACONS, READERS, (5) PSALMODISTS, THE PEOPLE* OF THE CITY OF PCHORAS* WITH NUBIA,* ITS NOME, BELOVED, SPIRITUAL CHILDREN, ABBA GABRIEL* IN THE LORD FATHER, GREETINGS (10) GABRIEL THE SERVANT OF JESUS CHRIST, BY THE GRACE OF GOD—

GLORY TO GOD ALWAYS AND FOR EVER (*Arabic*)

GLORY BELONGS TO GOD (*Coptic*)

—AND HIS INCOMPREHENSIBLE JUDGEMENTS, (15) THE ARCHBISHOP OF THE GREAT CITY OF RAKOTI AND BABYLON AND ITS TERRITORIES AND NUBIA AND THE ETHIOPIANS* AND THOSE WHICH ARE THEIRS, AND THE FIVE CITIES* WHICH ARE IN THE (20) WEST AND AFRICA.*

We inform you, O beloved, Orthodox, Christ's loving sons, the clergy, the priests, the deacons, and all the orders of the clergy, and the (25) elders, the archons, and all the Orthodox people, who are in the territory of the city of the Christ-loving Pchoras and Nubia and all its territories. May God bless them and keep them (30) and cause their possession to remain, and may He bless their habitations and their sons and their towns and their churches and every work in which they busy themselves, whether sowing or trading, and their crafts (35) and their means of nourishment and their lands, and may He save their souls with His strong arm and uplifted right hand, and may He give rest to every soul which has passed through the desert, and may He cause them to do that which pleases Him in (40) obedience, and may He strengthen them with one another in love and in the Orthodox Faith until the last breath, through the intercessions of the holy Mother of God, Saint Mary and the supplications of our holy Father (45) the Evangelist Mark and all the Holy Ones. Amen.

When God who is exalted willed to summon for you a bishop in the place of Abba Athanasios your father—Lord give rest (50) to his soul with His saints in the Paradise of joy—He was pleased to choose the beloved brother, the pious Christ-loving, good mild man, who is humble in consoling, who possesses the heart (55) which is free of wickedness, who possesses the spirit which is contrite, the one who fears God, and who walks in those things which please Him and who devotes himself to his appointment, who is full of the law and edification and tradition, the Orthodox Christ-loving (60) priest, who possesses the life worthy to be praised, Timotheos, according to that which is his own name.

This one became a priest and a monk over the Church* of the holy Mother of God (65) Saint Mary of Pchoras and Nubia. And we made him hegoumenos; and we have confirmed him as bishop over his province, the name of which we have already mentioned, on the day of the Lord's Day, which is the nineteenth day of the month of Athor, in the (70) 1088th year of the holy Martyrs, in the great Church* of the holy Mother of God Saint Mary, which is lifted up, in Fostat in Egypt, that which is guarded. When some of those who are our bishops (75) were present with the clergy and the elders, the archons who are honoured, and the Orthodox people—may God bless them with every heavenly blessing—(and) we fulfilled upon him the readings (80) which are proper and the laying on of hands, and we arrayed him in the garments of priesthood according to what is proper, and we gave to him the Rod of Iron,* in order that he should tend his people in the broad place of the pasture of (85) the Kingdom, and that he should protect them from the ravening wolves, and that he should nourish them with his apostolic teachings, and we called his name Abba Timotheos.

(90) And He who raises up a poor man from the dunghill has raised him up that he may sit with the rulers of his people. And the authority has befallen him through the grace which he has received from the Holy Spirit in order (95) that he may bind and that he may loose through the laying on of hands upon him, in order that he may consecrate new churches and altars, and ordain clergy freely just as he has received freely, (100) and do all the work which the bishops like him to do.

We have sent him to you after he has been changed, and has become even as a new man, full of all spiritual grace through (105) the gift which he has received. And as for the apostolic rank, he has received it, and it has become his own. It is proper for them and it is fitting for them to come out to meet him and to receive him to themselves in (110) honour and reverence and joy and gladness, and to submit to him, and to heed his words as Father and lord and master and priest of God and good teacher. He who heeds (115) him, me he heeds; and he who heeds me, Christ he heeds.

And you shall fulfil upon him the readings and the chapters through the brother bishops who come to you with him (120) according to the custom which is laid down, and to give to him those rights which are his together with his traditional dues, and to make him free of care in order that he for his part shall be at leisure to make intercession and to make supplication (125) for them day and night and to teach them concerning the salvation of their souls. Because the Holy Gospel says 'The labourer is worthy of his wage'.[1] The tongue of the sweet-smelling Paul says, (130) 'Who will tend a flock of sheep and he will not eat of its milk; or who is wont to plant a vineyard and he will not eat of its fruit?'[2] And, 'If we have sown for you spiritual things (135) what more is it that we reap of your bodily things?'[3] For the Lord has summoned him as a priest over them, just as the Apostle says, 'And no one is to receive this honour (to him) of his own self, but God has summoned him (140) like Aaron'.[4] David the Psalmist says 'Thou art the priest for ever according to the order of Melchziedek'.[5] We are not saying this to you as if we think of you as being (145) incomplete— God forbid; but we know that you are full of every spiritual grace—but to command ourselves to remind you and to teach you and to make you vigilant continually.

(150) May God the Word cause his coming and his reaching you to become for you a blessing upon your towns and your lands; and His peace and His confirming to remain upon His church (155) and all the inhabited world; and may He save our souls that we may bring heavenwards to Him the glory and the honour and the adoration with the Good Father and the Holy Spirit the

---

[1] Lk. x. 7   [2] I Cor. ix. 7   [3] I Cor. ix. 11   [4] Heb. v. 4   [5] Ps. cx. 4

Life-giver (and of the same substance with Him (160) now and for all times and for ever and all eternities. Amen.

This commendatory letter of our Father Abba Timotheos your Bishop we have confirmed with our own hands. (170) We have sent it with the most devout bishops who come to you with him in order to carry out by means of it his enthronement in the church of the bishops of the province.* Glory to the Lord for ever. Amen.

A. Witness of Michael, Bishop of Threbi (left upper)

In the name of the Holy Trinity, the Father, the Son and the Holy Spirit. The Poor man among the sons of men because (5a) of the multitude of his sins, even Michael of the see of Thribi and that which belongs to it was present at the laying of hands on our distinguished and honourable father the priest (10a) Timotheos, the man of Nubia by (his) birth, as hegemounos and for his office of bishop on the day of the Lord's Day the nineteenth day of the month of Athor in the year of the Martyrs 1088 in the holy (15a) Catholic Church of Saint Mary which is raised up, which is in Fostat of Egypt, by the hand of our father distinguished according to every excellence, (20a) the greatest of the Patriarchs, Abba Gabriel, the throne of the God-loving city of Rakoti and all the land (25a) of Egypt and the country of the Ethiopians and Nubia and the five cities which are in the West and all their territories. He ordained this priest as hegoumen and Bishop. (30a) And our father the Patriarch whose name we have already mentioned gave to him the name Timotheos, according to his name in the priesthood, over the throne of Apachoras (35a) which is in the country of Nubia. May the God of Heaven confirm our Patriarch Abba Gabriel upon his throne for many years and times of peace. Amen. (40a) May it be so. May it be so. The poor Michael wrote these lines on the 27th day of the month Athor in the year the name of which we have already mentioned. Lo I repent. (45a) Forgive me. In a peace of God. Amen.

B. Witness Peter, Bishop of Shmoun $\overline{B}$ = Ashmonein (right upper)

In the name of the Father and the Son and the Holy Spirit. The poor man of the sons of men (became) of his sins even Peter (5b) the Bishop of the Christ-loving city of Shmoun $\overline{B}$ and its provinces was present with those who were with him at the laying on of hands of our distinguished father the priest (10b) Timotheos, the man of Nubia by (his) birth and for his office of bishop in the day of the Lord's day in the nineteenth day of the month of Athor in the year of the martyrs 1088 in the Holy Catholic Apostolic Church of Saint Mary, (15b) which is lifted up, which is in Fostat of Egypt by the hand of our distinguished father the greatest of the Patriarchs, Abba Gabriel, the Patriarch upon (20b) the throne of Mark the Apostle, the throne of the city of the God-loving Rakoti and all the land of Egypt and the country of the Ethiopians and Nubia and the five cities which are in the west (25b) and all their territories. He ordained this priest as hegoumenos and bishop and gave him the name Timotheos, according to his name in the priesthood (30b) even our distinguished father the Patriarch, whose name we have already mentioned, upon the throne of Apachoras which is in the country of Nubia. May the God of Heaven confirm (35b) our distinguished father the Patriarch Abba Gabriel with many years and times of peace. Amen. So be it. So be it. (40b) The poor Peter wrote these lines, on the 27th day of this month of Athor in the year of which we have already mentioned its name. Lo, I repent. Forgive me. In a peace of God. Amen.

C. Witness of Mark, Bishop of Kebtō (left lower)

I was present, even I, the least (of men) Mark, the servant of the throne of the city of Kebtō and its territories, and the deputy of our father, Abba Gabriel (5c) the Patriarch of the great city of Alexandria and Egypt, Syria, Pentapolis, Africa and Nubia, Axum and Ethiopia on the throne of the city of Armonth and its territories, (10c) and I took part in the enthroning and the laying on of hands for our pious, thrice blessed and all virtuous father, our father Bishop Abba Timotheos, the Bishop (15c) of the city of the Christ-loving Apachoras of Nubia and its territories, in the company of our most pious and thrice blessed father Abba Athanasios, the bishop of the city (20c) of the God-loving Kosberber and its territories and the city of Armonth[1] and its territories, in the holy church of the saintly Martyr Victor in the monastery of the (25c) laura in the mountain of the desert of the west of Kamoule on the second holy Lord's day of the fast of the 40 holy days, the 20th day of the month of Mechir in the year 1088 of the (30c) Holy Martyrs. May their holy blessings be with us. Amen. May it be so (γενιτο). May it be so to the glory of God. Amen.

D. Witness of Athanasios, Bishop of Kosberbir (right lower)

God easy to reconcile

I was present, even I, Athanasios, the least of men, the servant of the throne of the city of Kosberbir and its territories, and the deputy of our father (5d) Abba Gabriel, Patriarch of the great city of Alexandria and Egypt and Pentapolis (and) Africa and Nubia, Axum and Ethiopia, (10d) on the throne of the city of Armonth and its territories. And I took part in the enthroning and the laying on of hands upon our most pious father (15d) (and) thrice blessed and all virtuous father, our father (and) Bishop Abba Timotheos the Bishop of the Christ-loving city of Apachoras of Nubia and its (20d) territories in company with our holy, most pious and thrice blessed father, Abba Mark the Bishop of the God-loving city of Kepto and its territories and the (25d) city of Kendore and its territories, in the holy Church (of) the Saintly Martyr Victor in the monastery of the laura in the mountain of the desert (30d) the West of Kamoule in the second Lord's day holy of (the fast of) the 40 holy days, the 20th day of the month Mechir the year 1088 of the holy Martyrs. May their (35d) holy blessings be with us. Amen. May it be so (γενιτο). May it be so to the glory of God. Amen.

Notes on the Coptic Scroll

The text of the Coptic Scroll is essentially the same as that contained in a fourteenth-century Coptic–Arabic manuscript in the Bibliothèque Nationale in Paris. This bilingual manuscript (Arab. 203) has been described as an encyclopedia of the ecclesiastical science of the Coptic Church. A section of the Arabic text was published by L. Villecourt in *Patrologia orientalis* 20 (1929). A table showing the main differences between the Scroll and the Paris MS. is set out on p. 17.

The first twenty lines of the Scroll are written in large ornamental characters. All the lines, with the exception of lines 2, 6, 11, 19 which are written in red ink, are in a thick black ink. The language of the first nine lines is Greek, but the spelling of the individual words and the syntax are so barbarously rendered that it must be supposed that the scribe's knowledge of Greek was infinitesimal. It is certain that the Scroll was copied from an exemplar itself already garbled, and possibly written

---

[1] Written ⲡⲙⲉⲛⲑ.

from dictation. Nevertheless, in spite of the errors the purport of the opening lines is obvious: a formal greeting from the Patriarch of Alexandria to the Christians of Nubia. For the reconstruction of the underlying Greek I am indebted to Dr. James Drescher.

τοῖς πᾶσι τοῦ θεοῦ φιλοχριστοτάτοις πρεσβυτέροις διακόνοις
ὑποδιακόνοις ἀναγνώσταις ψαλμῳδοῖς τῷ λαῷ τῆς πόλεως
Πεχωρας ⲛⲉⲙ ⲧⲗⲩⲃⲏ τοῦ νομοῦ αὐτῆς ἀγαπητοῖς πνευματικοῖς
τέκνοις ἀββᾶ Γαβριὴλ ἐν Κυρίῳ πατὴρ χαίρειν

Line 5: Drescher's suggestion that ⲧⲁⲁⲗⲱ is a misreading for ⲧⲱ ⲗⲁⲱ (τῷ λαῷ) is confirmed by the Paris MS. (fol. 166a).

Line 6: ⲡⲭⲱⲣⲁⲥ i.e. Faras, formerly the ecclesiastical centre of Nubia. By the fourteenth century Ibrîm had taken over both the name and the ecclesiastical functions of Faras. The transfer of the name to Ibrîm is attested in the Arabic counterpart of the Coptic Scroll, for though the Arabic form of Pachoras is given as the name of the see of the newly consecrated bishop, the Arabic name Ibrîm is in every case written in above. A number of funerary stelae of the bishops of Ibrîm, found in the recent excavations on the site, reveal that in the eleventh and twelfth centuries the place was known as Phrim. Notwithstanding the final abandonment of Faras, probably in the late twelfth century, the memory of this once great ecclesiastical centre lingered on for centuries in Nubia. Vansleb in his *Histoire de l'église d'Alexandrie*, 28 states, 'Dans la Nubie il y avoit autrefois, selon le même Mss cy-dessus cité (i.e. an old MS. shown to him by the Bishop of Asyût in 1673) trois Provinces, divissés en dix-sept Eveches. Dans la Province de Maraci il y avoit sept qui etoient 1. Celuy de Korta 2. d'Ibrim 3. de Bucoras 4. de Dunkala, qu'on prononce Dungala 5. de Sai 6. de Termus 7. de Scienkur.' According to the same writer, at the time when he was in Egypt the country was divided into twenty-four Casciefs of which the most southerly on the east bank of the Nile was the Casciaf of Ibrîm (*The Present State of Egypt* (London, 1678), 17). Ibrîm was at that time under the control of the garrison of Bosnian mercenaries who had been sent there by the Sultan Süleyman the Magnificent in 1528.

ⲛⲉⲙ ⲧⲗⲩⲃⲏ. A Coptic phrase inserted into the Greek text. ⲧⲗⲩⲃⲏ is the Coptic name for Nubia with the feminine definite article.

ⲗⲩⲃⲏ also appears in the Paris MS. For this name cf. H. Munier, *Recueil des listes épiscopales de l'église copte* (Cairo, 1943), 64, where there is the equivalence ⲧⲗⲩⲃⲏ النوبة (Al-Nūbah); also Vansleb, *Histoire de l'Église d'Alexandrie*, 29, 'la Nubie, appelée par les Coptes Lybie . . .'

Line 9: Gabriel IV was Patriarch from 1370 to 1378.

Line 18: ⲛⲓⲉⲑⲁⲩϣ. Probably here a reference to the inhabitants of modern Ethiopia.

Line 19. 'The five cities which are in the West', i.e. Barqa, the region of Cyrenaica.

Line 20: ⲫⲣⲓⲕⲓⲁ = the northern coast of Africa from Tripoli to Tunisia. The Paris MS. omits all reference to the Five Cities and Africa.

Line 64: For a reference to the Cathedral Church of St. Mary the Virgin at Ibrîm in the twelfth century, cf. Abu Saleh, *The Churches and the Monasteries of Egypt*, 266.

Line 71: The Church referred to here is the Church Al-Mu'allaqa or The Hanging Church in Old Cairo, at that time the seat of the Patriarchate.

Line 83: cf. Rev. ii, 27: 'And he shall rule them with a rod of iron'.

Lines 128–42: A comparison of the quotations from the Bible which appear in these lines with the Bohairic and Sahidic Versions is set out on p. 26.

Line 171: The Paris MS. reads here, 'We have sent to the most devout bishops that they should carry out his enthronement in the church in which the enthronement of the bishops is performed.' The different wording of this passage in Bishop Timotheos' document may reflect the prevailing circumstances in Nubia. It is possible that Timotheos could no longer depend on the attendance of local Nubian Bishops at his enthronement to carry out the necessary rites and ceremonies, but must await the availability of two bishops from Egypt to travel with him to Nubia. It is clear from the witness at the end of the Scrolls that circumstances were such that enthronement at Ibrîm proved impossible, and that after waiting three months he was formally enthroned in the Church of Apa Victor at Qamûla in Upper Egypt.

The Witnesses

For a valid performance of the rites and ceremonies for the consecration and enthronement of a bishop in the Coptic Church it was necessary that a fixed minimum number of bishops should be present on both occasions. It was also necessary that the bishops who were present at both ceremonies should confirm the fact of their attendance by adding to the Patriarch's Letters Testimonial a statement in their own handwriting. The form of this written testimonial was clearly based on an accepted mode. It is noteworthy that the form of witness appearing in the Coptic Scroll of Bishop Timotheos is considerably longer and more detailed than the model form which is to be found in the Paris MS. It is further to be noted that each of the four bishops who witnessed Timotheos' Scrolls were able to write in Coptic and in Arabic. One bishop, Athanasios of Qûṣ, was able to add a postscript to his Coptic witness in passable Greek.

Two of the bishops, Michael of Athribis and Peter of Ashmûnein, testified that they were present at Timotheos' consecration in the famous Hanging Church of St. Mary in Old Cairo on Sunday, 19th Hathor in the year of the Martyrs 1088 (A.D. 1371–2). From the witness of both these bishops we learn that Timotheos was a Nubian by race. In the Coptic Scroll his see is described as Apachoras which is in the country of Nubia. In the Arabic counterpart the name of Timotheos' see is written as Abakyras, the equivalent of the Coptic Apachoras, and the name Ibrîm is written in above—an obvious insertion. The witness of both bishops is dated Monday, 27th Hathor, eight days after the actual consecration. This lapse of time must be accounted for by the period of time needed for the preparation of the elaborate Letters Testimonial.

The written testimony of the remaining bishops who witnessed, Mark of Qifṭ (who was in charge of the see of Dendera) and Athanasios of Qûṣ (who was in charge of the see of Armant), reveals that they were only present at the rite of the enthronement of Timotheos. Furthermore, their testimony shows that the enthronement did not take place, as might have been assumed, in the Cathedral Church at Ibrîm but three months after Timotheos' consecration in the Church of the Martyr St. Victor at Qamûla near the modern Naqâda. As has already been observed, conditions in Nubia may have been the reason for the delay of three months and the eventual enthronement in Upper Egypt. It is also not impossible that the Cathedral at Ibrîm was at that time in too ruinous a state to allow of a proper performing of the rites and ceremonies of the enthronement. Against this it should be pointed out that there is some evidence in connection with the blocking of the stairway, which led down to the place where Timotheos was buried, to suggest that at the time of Timotheos' consecration the Cathedral was in a reasonable state of repair.

Notes on the Witnesses' Autographs in the Coptic Scroll

A 6: ⲟⲣⲉⲃⲓ. The Arabic counterpart confirms that this is the town in the Delta, the ancient *Ḥwt-tꜣ-ḥr-ib*, the Greek Ἀθρῖβις and the Arabic أتريب now تل أتريب. In the Arabic Scroll there is mention of the famous Church of St. Mary the Virgin at Athribis (cf. Amélineau, *Géog.*, 66). It would seem from this mention that that Church was still standing in A.D. 1372.

B 6: ϣⲙⲟⲩⲛ ⲃ̄ = the ancient Hermopolis, now the modern El-Ashmûnein. On the form of the name in Coptic cf. Amélineau, *Géog.*, 167–8, and Quatremère, *Mém. Géog.* i. 498.

C 3: ⲕⲉⲃⲧⲱ = the ancient Coptos, now the modern Qifṭ. Cf. Amélineau, op. cit. 213.

C 9: ⲁⲣⲙⲟⲛⲑ = Armant (cf. Amélineau, op. cit. 165–6). The statement here in the third letter that Armant was under the charge of Mark the Bishop of Qifṭ is clearly a mistake, for the next witness, Athanasios of Qûṣ, states quite clearly in both the Coptic and the Arabic Scrolls that Mark was in charge of the See of Dendera, and that he himself was over the See of Armant.

D 4: ⲕⲱⲥ ⲃⲉⲣⲃⲓⲣ = the modern Qûṣ. On the form of the name cf. Amélineau, op. cit. 399–400.

D 25: ⲕⲉⲛⲧⲱⲣⲉ = the modern Dendera, the Classical Tentyris or Tentyra, and the Coptic ⲛ̄ⲧⲉⲛⲧⲱⲣⲓ. For the variant spellings of this name cf. Amélineau, op. cit. 141.

The Greek Postscript (Pl. XIV)

At the end of his autograph in Coptic Bishop Athanasios added eight lines of Greek. The content of this postscript is a summary of his Coptic autograph. Unfortunately, since the postscript was written at the very end of the scroll, it has suffered some damage. There are a number of breaks in the paper, and only one line of writing is now entire. Why Athanasios should have added this short passage in Greek is not clear. It is possible that he wished to do no more than show off his knowledge of Greek. On the other hand it is just possible that the Nubian Church was still preserving its ancient practice of using Greek for the liturgy, in which case Athanasios' note may have been an acknowledgement of the continuance of that tradition. Whatever was the reason, it is remarkable to find the knowledge of the Greek language still surviving in the Nile Valley in the late fourteenth century. The diplomatic transcript below is followed by the text in modern form.

```
1            ]θϲ[        ]ακ[. .]ν
                          χ υ
2      . . υναχθωεγωελααθανασιοϲ [
        σ        ε  ι              λ
3      ο ‾ πολεωϲκωϲβρβρκτωνοριωναυτη[
        φ
4      α εκτουθρονιϲμουτουπρϲημωναββατιμοθεου[
        τ
5      ε τηϲϲλταπαχωραϲτηϲλυβηϲκτωνοριωναυτηϲ · εντη
6      θ αγ[. .]εκκληϲιατουαγ.[   ] . . .[.]βικτωρο[.]τουμοναϲτηριο[
        ε
7      α λαυραορηπεχουε ορηκαμ[.] . . [   ]τ[   ] . .[   ] .[
        μ
8      η δευτερηεκτηϲαγιαϲνηϲτιαϲκμεν‾ⲟ̄ⲥμε[
```

```
1            θ(εὸ)ς [εὐδιαλλ]ακ[τό]ν.
2      . . υναχθῶ ἐγὼ ἐλάχ(ιστος) Ἀθανάσιος [δοῦλος τοῦ θρόνου τῆς]
3      πόλεως Κῶς Βερβὶρ κ(αὶ) τῶν ὁρίων αὐτῆ[ς                    ]
4      ἐκ τοῦ θρονισμοῦ τοῦ π(ατ)ρ(ὸ)ς ἡμῶν Ἀββᾶ Τιμοθέου [ἐπισκόπου]
5      τῆς πόλεως Ἀπαχώρας τῆς Λύβης κ(αὶ) τῶν ὁρίων αὐτῆς · ἐν τῇ
6      ἁγί[ᾳ] ἐκκλησίᾳ τοῦ ἁγί[ου μάρτυ]ρ[ος] Βίκτωρο[ς] τοῦ μοναστηρίο[υ]
7      λαύρα ὄρη Πεχουε ὄρη Καμ[ο]υλ[ε    ἐν] τ[ῇ ἁγί]ᾳ κ[υ]ρ[ιακῇ τῇ]
8      δευτέρη ἐκ τῆς ἁγίας νηστίας κ̄ μενὸς Με[χίρ, ἔτους ϡπη ἀπὸ μαρτύρων]
9      δόξα τῷ θ(ε)ῷ ἀμήν.
```

Translation

God easy to reconcile

Glory to God Amen

I, even I the least of men, Athanasios (the servant of the throne of)
the city of Kos Berbir and its territories (   )
attended for the enthroning of our father, Abba Timotheos the Bishop
of the city of Apachoras of Nubia and its territories in the
holy Church of the Holy Martyr Victor of the Monastery
and laura in the mountain (. . . . . . . Kamouli (?) . . . on the holy Sunday)
the second in the Holy Fast the 20th day of the month of Mechir (Year 1088 of the Martyrs)

Notes

Line 1: θεος ευδιαλλακτον ^{sic} restored by analogy with the opening words of the Coptic autograph.

Line 2: Before υναχθω the writing is damaged and the traces not clear, but it can hardly be doubted that συναχθω was either written or intended. In form συναχθῶ. is the 1st person singular, aorist subjunctive passive of συνάγειν, but there is no construction for a subjunctive here, and it becomes necessary, if Greek syntax is to be imposed, to correct it to the indicative, συνήχθην. According to the Greek Patristic Lexicon the passive, συνάγεσθαι, used intransitively, can mean to gather or assemble for worship, to join in corporate worship, or to be present at the Eucharist. In the present context it clearly means 'I was present', i.e. at the Institution of the Bishop.

συνάγειν was taken over into Coptic with much the same range of meanings as in Greek: for definitions and a selection of examples see *ZÄS* 96, 1969, p. 80.

In the lacuna at the end of the line δοῦλος τοῦ θρόνου has been restored as the equivalent of the Coptic; ἐπίσκοπος would be too short for the available space.

Line 3: Some verb meaning 'I took part in', as in the Coptic, is required in the lacuna at the end of the line, e.g. συμμετέσχον.

Line 4: The preposition ἐκ is improperly used, as also in line 8.

Line 7: What appears to be the trace of a letter preceding λαύρα is probably part of the *alpha* at the beginning of the line above.

Πεχουε, which is a reasonably certain reading, is presumably intended as a Greek rendering of a Coptic place name. It is possible that the same Coptic word appears in the Arabic scroll in the form Bishulu (cf. p. 37).

After ὄρη, καμ[ο]υλε suits such traces as can be distinguished, though the writing is severely damaged. Whether this was followed in the lacuna by some Greek equivalent of 'West', as in the Coptic, is uncertain. ἐν τῇ ἁγίᾳ κυριακῇ is restored from the Coptic.

Line 8: The preposition ἐκ is superfluous, as in line 4. At the end of the line ἔτους ϥπη ἀπὸ μαρτύρων has been restored as there is clearly no room for τῶν ἁγίων μαρτύρων, as in the Coptic. The shorter wording was necessitated by lack of space, for Athanasius had come to the bottom of the scroll. This no doubt also explains the omission of, e.g., γένοιτο, and the fact that δόξα τῷ θεῷ ἀμήν had to be written vertically in the left-hand margin of the scroll.

Timotheos' enthronement was carried out on the second Sunday of the Lenten Fast in Year 1088 of the Era of the Martyrs (which ran from 30 August 1371 to 28 August 1372). The Copts have an extra Sunday in Lent, equivalent to Quinquagesima, our last Sunday before Lent; so their second Sunday in Lent corresponds with our first Sunday in Lent. In A.D. 1372 this second Sunday fell on 20 Mechir (=15 February), as stated here. Easter Day fell on 2 Pharmouthi (= 28 March) in 1372, see V. Grumel, *Traité d'études byzantines*, I. *La chronologie* (Paris, 1958), 261. The extra Coptic Sunday in Lent is explained on p. 333 of the same work.

The Scriptural Citations in the Coptic Scroll

Comparison of the citations of scripture in the Coptic Scroll with the Bohairic version of the New Testament shows that in a few instances the citations agree with the Sahidic version against the Bohairic. It is not impossible, therefore, that an earlier redaction of the Bohairic text was in use when the original exemplar of the Letter Testimonial was drawn up, or that the whole Letter is a translation into Bohairic from a Sahidic original. This latter possibility, if proven, would be a testimony to the antiquity of the practice of sending such Letters Testimonial by the Patriarch to the people of a diocese when a new bishop was consecrated to the See.

The Bohairic text is taken from Horner's edition. The Sahidic text is also taken from Horner's edition supplemented by Thompson's edition of the Pauline Epistles based on the Chester Beatty MS. in Dublin.

Bishop Timotheos' Scroll	The Bohairic Version	The Sahidic Version
l. 128 — Lk. x. 7		
ⲡⲓⲉⲣⲅⲁⲧⲏⲥ ϥⲉⲙⲡϣⲁ ⲛ̇ⲧⲉϥϧⲣⲉ	ⲡⲓⲉⲣⲅⲁⲧⲏⲥ ⲅⲁⲣ ϥⲙⲡϣⲁ ⲛ̇ⲧⲉϥϧⲣⲉ[1]	ⲡⲉⲣⲅⲁⲧⲏⲥ ⲅⲁⲣ ⲙ̅ⲡϣⲁ ⲙ̅ⲡⲉϥⲃⲉⲕⲉ
ll. 131–4 — I Cor. ix. 7		
ⲛⲓⲙ ⲉⲑⲛⲁⲁⲙⲟⲛⲓ ⲛ̇ⲟⲩⲟϩⲓ ⲛ̇ⲉⲥⲱⲟⲩ ⲟⲩⲟϩ ⲛ̇ⲧⲉϥϣⲧⲉⲙⲟⲩⲱⲙ ⲉⲃⲟⲗ ϧⲉⲛ ⲡⲉϥⲉⲣⲱϯ ⲓⲉ ⲛⲓⲙ ⲉϣⲁϥϭⲟ ⲛ̇ⲟⲩ ⲓⲁϩⲁⲗⲟⲗⲓ ⲟⲩⲟϩ ⲛ̇ⲧⲉϥϣⲧⲉⲙⲟⲩⲱⲙ ⲉⲃⲟⲗ ϧⲉⲛⲡⲉϥⲟⲩⲧⲁϩ	ⲛⲓⲙ ⲉϣⲁϥⲙⲟⲛⲓ ⲛ̇ⲟⲩⲟϩⲓ ⲛ̇ⲉⲥⲱⲟⲩ (ⲟⲩⲟϩ) ⲛ̇ⲧⲉϥϣⲧⲉⲙⲟⲩⲱⲙ ⲉⲃⲟⲗ ϧⲉⲛ ⲡⲉⲣⲱϯ ⲛ̇ⲧⲉⲡⲓⲟϩⲓ ⲛⲓⲙ ⲉϣⲁϥϭⲟ ⲛ̇ⲟⲩ ⲓⲁϩⲁⲗⲟⲗⲓ ⲟⲩⲟϩ ⲙ̇ⲡⲁϥⲟⲩⲱⲙ ⲉⲃⲟⲗ ϧⲉⲛⲡⲉϥⲟⲩⲧⲁϩ[2]	ⲛⲓⲙ ⲡⲉϣⲁϥⲙⲟⲟⲛⲉ ⲛ̅ⲟⲩⲟϩⲉ ⲛ̅ϥ̅ⲧⲙ̅ⲟⲩⲱⲙ ⲙ̅ⲡⲉϥⲉⲣⲱⲧⲉ . . . ⲛⲓⲙ ⲡⲉϣⲁϥⲧⲱϭⲉ ⲛ̅ⲟⲩ ⲙⲁ ⲛ̅ⲉⲗⲟⲟⲗⲉ ⲛ̅ϥ̅ⲧⲙ̅ⲟⲩⲱⲙ ⲙ̅ⲡⲉϥⲕⲁⲣⲡⲟⲥ[2]
ll. 135–6 — I Cor. ix. 11		
ⲓⲥⲭⲉ ⲁⲛⲥⲓϯ ⲛⲱⲧⲉⲛ ⲛ̇ϩⲁⲛⲡⲛ̅ⲁ̅ ⲧⲓⲕⲟⲛ ⲟⲩϩⲟⲩⲟ ⲡⲉ ⲭⲉ ⲛ̇ⲧⲉⲛ ⲱⲥϧ ⲛ̇ⲛⲉⲧⲉⲛⲥⲁⲣⲕⲓⲕⲟⲛ	ⲓⲥⲭⲉ ⲁⲛⲟⲛ ⲁⲛⲥⲓϯ ⲛⲱⲧⲉⲛ ⲛ̇ⲛⲓ ⲡ̅ⲛ̅ⲁ̅ⲧⲓⲕⲟⲛ ⲟⲩⲛⲓϣϯ ⲡⲉ ⲉϣⲱⲡ ⲁⲛ ϣⲁⲛⲱⲥϧ ⲛ̇ⲧⲉⲛⲥⲁⲣⲕⲓⲕⲟⲛ	ⲉϣⲭⲉ ⲁⲛⲟⲛ ⲁⲛⲭⲟ ⲛⲏⲧⲛ̅ ⲛ̅ⲡⲉ ⲡⲛⲉⲩⲙⲁⲧⲓⲕⲟⲛ ⲟⲩⲛⲟϭ ⲡⲉ ⲉϣⲭⲉ ⲁⲛⲟⲛ ⲡⲉⲧⲛⲁⲱϩⲥ̅ ⲛ̅ⲡⲉⲧⲛ̅ⲥⲁⲣⲕⲓⲕⲟⲛ
ll. 139–41 — Heb. v. 4		
ⲟⲩⲟϩ ⲙ̇ⲡⲁⲣⲉⲟⲩⲁⲓϭⲓ ⲛⲁϥ ⲙ̇ⲡⲓ ⲧⲁⲓⲟ ⲙ̇ⲙⲁⲩⲁⲧϥ ⲁⲗⲗⲁ ⲁϥⲑⲱϩⲉⲙ ⲙ̇ⲙⲟϥ ⲛ̇ϫⲉϥϯ ⲙ̇ⲫⲣⲏϯ ⲛ̇ⲁⲁⲣⲱⲛ	ⲟⲩⲟϩ ⲙ̇ⲡⲁⲣⲉⲟⲩⲁⲓϭⲓ ⲛⲁϥ ⲙ̇ⲡⲓ ⲧⲁⲓⲟ ⲙ̇ⲙⲁⲩⲁⲧϥ ⲁⲗⲗⲁ ⲁϥⲑⲱϩⲉⲙ ⲙ̇ⲙⲟϥ ⲛ̇ϫⲉϥϯ ⲕⲁⲧⲁⲫⲣⲏϯ ⲛ̇ⲁⲁⲣⲱⲛ	ⲡⲉⲣⲉⲡⲟⲩⲁ ⲇⲉ ⲡⲟⲩⲁϫⲓ [ⲛⲁϥ][3] ⲁⲛ ⲙ̅ⲡⲧⲁⲓⲟ ⲁⲗⲗⲁ ⲉⲩⲧⲱⲣⲙ̅[4] ⲙ̅ⲙⲟⲩ ⲉⲃⲟⲗ ϩⲓⲧⲙ̅ⲡⲛⲟⲩⲧⲉ (ⲛ)ⲕⲁⲧⲁⲑⲉ ⲛ̅ⲁⲁⲣⲱⲛ
ll. 142–4 — Heb. v. 6 (Ps. cx. 4)		
ⲛ̇ⲑⲟⲕ ⲡⲉϥⲟⲩⲏⲃ ϣⲁⲉⲛⲉϩ ⲕⲁⲧⲁ ⲧⲧⲁⲍⲓⲥ ⲙ̇ⲙⲉⲗⲭⲓⲥⲉⲇⲉⲕ	ⲛ̇ⲑⲟⲕ ⲡⲉϥⲟⲩⲏⲃ ϣⲁⲉⲛⲉϩ ⲕⲁⲧⲁ ⲧⲧⲁⲍⲓⲥ ⲙ̇ⲙⲉⲗⲭⲓⲥⲉⲇⲉⲕ	ⲛ̅ⲧⲟⲕ ⲡⲉ ⲡⲟⲩⲏⲏⲃ ϣⲁⲉⲛⲉϩ ⲕⲁⲧⲁ ⲧⲧⲁⲍⲓⲥ ⲙ̅ⲙⲉⲗⲭⲓⲍⲉⲇⲉⲕ

[1] Half the Boh. MSS. read ⲃⲉⲭⲉ.

[2] The order of the phrases is inverted, as in the text of the Scroll.

[3] ⲛⲁϥ is attested only in the Chester Beatty MS.

[4] For ⲧⲱⲣⲙ the Chester Beatty MS. reads ⲉⲓⲛⲉ.

PART 3

THE ARABIC SCROLL

(Cairo 90224)

Arabic Text[1]

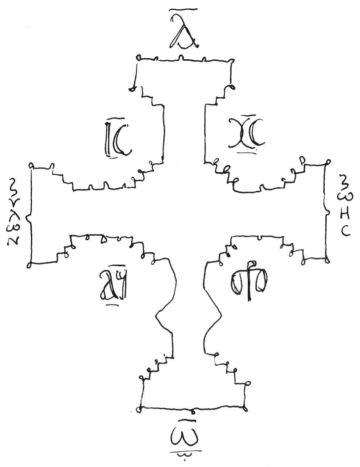

بسم الأب والابن والروح القدس الإله الواحد

من غبريال عبد يسوع المسيح بنعمة الله وأحكامه غير المدركة

المجد لله دائما أبدا

ⲠⲒϢⲞⲨ ⲪⲀϤϮ ⲠⲈ

رئيس أساقفة المدينة العظمى الإسكندرية ومصر وأعمالها ٥

²والحبشة والنوبة وما جمع إليها نعلمكم أيها الأولاد الأحباء

الأرثدكسيين محبى المسيح الكهنة القسوس والشمامسة وجميع

رتب الكهنوت والشيوخ الأراخنة وكل الشعب الأرثدكسى

وإبريم

أباخراس من أعمال النوبة المرسوم بكنيسة الست السيدة وبالرسل

وما جمع إليها الله يبارك عليهم ويحفظهم ويطيل أعمارهم ويديم ١٠

عزهم ويبارك على منازلهم وبلدانهم وكنائسهم وزرعاتهم

وتجاراتهم وصناعاتهم ويبارك على مواشيهم وجميع

ما يتقلبون فيه ويحرسهم بيمينه الحصين وذراعه القوى

---

[1] Diacritical points, hamzas, and maddas have been added where appropriate; short vowel signs have been omitted. Otherwise, orthographical idiosyncrasies and grammatical irregularities are given as found. ² Line written in red.

ويخلص نفوسهم وينيح نفوس أسلافهم ويمنحهم أن يعملوا

١٥ بمرضاته ويثبتهم فى الأمانة الأرثدكسية إلى النفس الأخير
بشفاعة سيدتنا والدة الإله القديسة الطاهرة مرتمريم البتول
وأبينا مرقس الإنجيلى الرسول وجميع القديسين آمين .
إنه لما أراد الرب أن يدعوا١ لهم أسقفا عوضا عن أنبا أثناسيوس
الأسقف كان نيح الله نفسه سر أن يختار الأخ الحبيب

٢٠ العابد المحب للمسيح الصالح الوديع المتواضع المعزى
صاحب القلب السليم والروح المنسحقة الخائف من الله
الماشى فى مرضاته الساعى فى سبله الممدوح السيرة النقى السريرة
المملوا٢ ناموسا وتبيانا الأرثدكسى الراهب القس المكرم طيموثاوس
من أجل أنه مستحقا لهذه الرئاسة أقسمناه أغومنسا وكملناه أسقفا على الكراسى

٢٥ المقدم ذكرها فى يوم الأحد تاسع عشر هاتور سنة ثمانية٣ وثمانين وألف لشهداء الأطهار
فى الكنيسة الكبرى التى للسيدة الطاهرة مرتمريم البتول المعلقة بفسطاط
مصر المحروسة بحضور بعض الأساقفة والكهنة والشيوخ الأجلاء الأراخنة والشعب
الأرثدكسى الرب يبارك عليهم بكل البركات السمائية وكملنا عليه الصلوات
اللائقة بالتكريز وألبسناه الثياب الكهنوتية كما يجب وأعطيناه العكاز

٣٠ الجديد ليرعى شعبه فى المرج الخصيب الملوكى ويحفظهم من الذئاب الخاطفة
وينيرهم من التعاليم الرسولية ودعونا اسمه طيموثاوس كما كان أولا ورفعه الذى
يرفع الفقير من الزبالة ليجلس مع رؤساء شعبه وصار له السلطان من قبل النعمة
التى نالها من الروح القدس بوضع اليد أن يحل ويربط ويكرز الكنائس والهياكل الجدد
ويقسم الكهنة مجانا كما أخذ مجانا ويعمل جميع ما تعمله الأساقفة أمثاله وأرسلناه

٣٥ إليكم من بعد ما تبدل وصار إنسانا جديدا مملوا٤ من كل حكمة ونعمة روحانية من قبل النعمة التى
نالها والدرجة الابسطلية التى تسلمها وصارت إليه فينبغى لهم ويجب عليهم أن يستقبلوه
ويقبلوه بإكرام وفرح وابتهاج وخضوع وأن يسمعوا كلامه كالأب والسيد والمالك وكاهن الله
والمعلم الصالح فمن سمع منه فقد سمع منى ومن سمع منى فقد سمع من المسيح فتكملوا عليه
الفصول التى للقسمة على يدى الإخوة الأساقفة الواصلين إليكم معه كجارى العادة

٤٠ وليعط حقوقه ورسومه حتى يكون بغير اهتمام ويصير متفرغا للصلاة والطلبة عنهم فى
الليل والنهار ويعلمهم خلاص نفوسهم لأن الإنجيل المقدس يقول إن الاجير مستحق لطعامه
ويقول بولس الرسول من الذى يرعى غنما ولا يأكل من لبن رعيته أو من الذى يغرس
كرما ولا يأكل من ثمرته وقال أيضا إن كنا قد زرعنا فيكم الروحانيات
أعظيم هو أن نحصد فيكم الجسدانيات لأن الرب دعاه كاهنا عليهم كما يقول الرسول

٤٥ إنه ليس احد يأخذ الكرامة لنفسه إلا أن يدعوه الله مثل هرون وأيضا المرتل داود يقول
إنك أنت الكاهن إلى الأبد على طقس ملشيصداق ولم نقل هذا لأنكم ناقصون بل نحن نعلم
أنكم ممتلئون من كل نعمة روحانية وقد أمرنا أن نذكركم ونعلمكم ونبقطكم٥ دائما
والله الكلمة يجعل مجيئه٦ ووصوله إليكم يكون بالبركة والكرامة عليكم أنتم وأولادكم

ويجعـل السـلامـة والطمـأنـينـة دائـمة فى بيعتكم وفى كل المسكونة ويخـلـص نفوسنا

50 جميعا لتقدم له الشكر والكرامة والسجود مع أبيه الصالح والروح القدس المحيى المساوى

معه الآن وكل أوان وإلى دهر الداهرين آمين .

سـلام الـرب الـحـال عـلى تـلانـيـذه الأطـهـار وقديسيه الأبرار يـحل علـيـه

وعـلـيـهـم ونـعـمـتـه وبـركـتـه تـكـون مـعـهـم آمـيـن .

هذه الرسالة السيسطاديكى أى التقليد الذى لـلأب الفاضل

55 أنبا طيموثاوس أسقفهم تبنّاها[1] بخط أيدينا وأرسلناها إلى

الإخوة الأساقفة ليحضروا تجليسه على كراسيه فى البيعة التى

يجلس فيها أساقفة الكرسى . والمجد والشكر لله دائما أبـدا

والسبح لله دائما أبدا

A

بسم الله الرؤوف الرحيم

حضر التـلـميـذ المـسكين بذنـوبه أقل خلـق الله ميخائيـل بكنيسة

الـسـت السـيـدة بـاتـريب وبا مـعـها تكريـز الأب القـديـس

الـرئـيـس الأفـضـل فى أبـنـاء جنـسـه القس طيـمـاثاوس النـوبى

أسقفا على كرسى ابكيراس وإبريم مـن أعمال النوبة فى اليوم التاسع عشر

5 مـن هتـور يوم الأحد المبارك* بالكنيسة المعظمة المعلقة بفسطاط

مـصر مـن اليـد الطـاهـرة الأبـويـة السـيـديـة البـطـريـركـية

الـغـبـريـلـية بطريرك المـديـنـة العـظـمى الإسكـندرية والديار المصرية

والـحبشـية والـنـوبية والخـمس المدن الغـربـية وبا نسـب الى ذلك

الـرب الإلـه يـديـم بدوام السـلامـة والطمـأنـيـنة أيـامـه لـلـشعب الأرثدكسى

10 بالكرسى المرقسى آمين يـوم الإثنين سابع وعشرين هتور كتب هذه الاحرف

رزقنا الله بركاتهم آمين   الحقير بذنوبه ميخائيل الراجى عفو الله ورحمته والسبح لله دائما

B

بسم الله الرؤوف الرحيم

حضر التـلـميـذ المـسكين بذنـوبه أقل خلق الله بطرس

خادم كرسى مدينة الأشمونين وبا معها ونسب إليـها تكريز

الأب القديس الرئـيـس الأفضل فى أبناء جنسه القس

5 طيماثاوس النوبى أسقفا على كرسى أبكيراس وإبريم من أعمال

وثمانٍ وثمانين .leg [2]   ثبتناها .leg [1]

النوبة فى اليوم التاسع عشر من هتور يوم الأحد المبارك

من سنين ألف وثمانية وثمانون[1] للشهداء الأبرار

بالكنيسة المعظمة بفسطاط مصر من اليد الطاهرة

الأبوية السيدية البطريركية الغبريلية بطريرك

المدينة العظما الإسكندرية والديار المصرية والحبشية ١٠

والنوبية والخمس مدن الغربية وما نسب الى ذلك

الرب الإله يديم [بدوام][2] السلامة والطمأنينة أيامه للشعب

الأرثدكسى بالكرسى المرقسى آمين يوم الإثنين سابع

وعشرين هتور سنة ألف ثمانية[3] وثمانين   كتب هذه الأحرف

رزقنا الله بركاتهم آمين   الحقير بذنوبه بطرس الراجى عفو الله ١٥

ورحمته   والسبح لله دائما

C

حضرت نا الحقير بخطاياى البائس بذنوبى أحقر بنى البشر مرقس عبد المسيح خادم

كرسى قفط وما ينسب اليها شرقا وغربا بنعمة الله وأحكامه الغير مدركة رافع

الفقير من المزبلة ويجلسه[4] مع رؤساء شعبه والمفوض له آنئذ النيابة عن القلاية

المعمورة السيدية الأبوية البطريركية الغبريلية أدام الله تعميرها [ببقاء][5] مالكها ورزق

الكافة بركة صلوات ساكنيها آمين تجليس الأب السيد الطاهر الطوبانى الملاك ٥

الجسدانى والإنسان الروحانى المكرم الأسقف أنبا طيماثاوس أسقف كرسى

أبوخراس وإبريم وما ينسب إليه عرفا وشهرة وشاركت فى التجليس المبارك

المذكور ووضع اليد والأكسيوس مع الأب السيد الطاهر المعلم الماهر الراعى

الصالح والتاجر الرابح الأسقف المكرم أنبا أثناسيوس أسقف كرسى مدينة قوص

وما ينسب إليها شرقا وغربا والنائب على كرسى مدينة أرمنت أدام الله تعميره ١٠

بكنيسة الشاهد الكريم مار بقطر [بديره][6] المعروف بدير الكولة بجبل بشولو بحاجر غرب قمولة

وذلك فى الأحد الثانى من الصيام المقدس العشرين من شهر أمشير سنة ثمان وثمانين

وألف للشهداء الأطهار رزقنا الله بركاتهم آمين والسبح لله دائما أبدا

D

الله الحسن اللطف

حضرت أنا الحقير بخطاياى البائس بذنوبى أحقر بنى البشر أثناسيوس عبد المسيح

وخادمهم بكرسى مدينة قوص المحروسة وأعمالها شرقا وغربا بنعمة الله وأحكامه الغير مدركة

رافع الفقير من المزبلة وبجلسه مع رؤساء شعبه والمفوض له آنئذ النيابة عن القلاية

المعمورة الأبوية السيدية البطريركية الغبريلية أدام الله تعميرها ببقاء مالكها ورزق الكافة بركة ٥

<hr>

1-1 leg. من سنة ألف وثمانٍ وثمانين

2 Added on the basis of A, line 10.

3 leg. وثمانٍ

4 Cf. D, line 4 — وبجلسه

5 Added on the basis of D, line 5.

6 Added on the basis of D, line 11.

صلوات ساكنها آمين على كرسى مدينة أرمنت وما ينسب اليها شرقا وغربا كما كان أيضا فى

الأيام الأبوية السيدية البطريركية البولسية المعمدة تلك النفس الطاهرة الزكية بالنياح السرمدي

فى الأماكن النورانية بمشيئة الله تعالى تجليس الأب السيد الطاهر الطوبانى الملك

الجسدانى الإنسان الروحانى الأسقف المكرم أنبا طيماثاوس أسقف كرسى أبوخراس

١٠ وإبريم وما نسب اليه عرفا وشهرة وشاركت فى التجليس المبارك المذكور ووضع

اليد والأكسيوس مع الأب السيد الطاهر المعلم الماهر الراعى الصالح التاجر

الرابح الأسقف المكرم أنبا مرقس أسقف كرسى مدينة قفط وما ينسب إليها شرقا وغربا

والنائب على كرسى مدينة دندرة وما ينسب إليها شرقا وغربا أدام الله تعميره بكنيسة

الشاهد الكريم مار بقطر بديره المعروف بدير الكولة بجبل بشولو

١٥ بحاجر غرب قمولة وذلك فى الأحد الثانى من الصيام المقدس العشرين من

شهر أمشير سنة ثمان وثمنين وألف للشهداء الأطهار رزقنا الله بركاتهم آمين

والسبح لله دائما سرمدا

Translation of Arabic Scroll

* Indicates a note on p. 37

In the name of the Father, and the Son and the Holy Ghost, one God
From Gabriel the servant of Jesus Christ, by the grace of God and His inscrutable judgements
Glory be to God always and for ever (*Arabic*)
Glory belongs to God (*Coptic*)

(5) The head of the bishops of the great city of Alexandria, Miṣr and its provinces, and Ethiopia and Nubia and what belongs to them. We inform you, our beloved Orthodox sons, lovers of Christ, the clergy, priests, deacons, all the orders of the clergy, the elders [who are] the archons* and all the orthodox people [of] Abâkhirâs and Ibrîm of the provinces of Nubia who are subject to the decree of the Church of the Lady and the Apostles (10) and what belongs to them (scil. the provinces). May God bless them, preserve them and prolong their lives, perpetuate their might and bless their habitations, towns, churches, plantations, trades, handicrafts and bless their livestock and everything in which they engage. May God guard them with his strong right hand and his powerful arm, save their souls, give rest to the souls of their ancestors, grant that they do (15) what pleases Him, and strengthen them in the Orthodox faith till the last breath, by the intercession of our Lady, the Pure Holy Mother of God, Saint Mary the Virgin, and of our Father Mark the Evangelist and Apostle and of all the saints. Amen.

33

When the Lord wished to summon for them a bishop instead of Anbâ Athanâsyûs the bishop—may God have given rest to his soul—He was pleased to choose the beloved brother, (20) the devoted, the lover of Christ, the upright, the meek, the humble, the consoler, who has a sound heart and a contrite spirit, fears God, walks in what is pleasing to Him, goes in His paths, is praised in his way of life, is pure in heart, is filled with law [of God] and with [the ability of] making [its] meaning clear, the Orthodox, the monk, the honoured priest Ṭîmûthâ'us.

Because he is worthy of this leadership, we have ordained him hegumen* and made him bishop over the above mentioned (25) sees on Sunday the nineteenth of Hatûr, in the year 1088 [in the era] of the Pure Martyrs, in the great church which is [dedicated] to the Pure Lady, Saint Mary the Virgin, [namely] al-Muʿallaqa* in Fusṭâṭ of Miṣr the guarded, in the presence of some of the bishops, the clergy, the great elders [who are] the archons, and the Orthodox people, may God bless them with all heavenly blessings. And we have fulfilled over him the proper prayers of consecration and we have clothed him with the clerical vestments as is incumbent and we have given him the new (30) staff,* in order that he may tend his people in the royal fertile pasture, to keep them from the ravening wolves and enlighten them with apostolic teachings. And we have called his name Ṭîmûthâ'us, as it was first.

And He who raises up the poor man from the refuse has raised him up to sit among the chiefs of his people, and he has obtained the authority—through the grace he has received from the Holy Spirit by the laying of hands—to loose, to bind, to consecrate new churches and altars, to ordain clergy freely just as he has taken freely, and to do all that the bishops like him do.

We have sent him (35) to you after he has been changed and has become a new man, full of all wisdom and spiritual grace, through the grace which he has acquired and the apostolic* rank which he has received and [which] has come to him. So it is fitting for them and incumbent upon them to receive him and accept him with honour, joy, gladness and submission and to hear his words as a father, lord, master, priest of God and upright teacher—whosoever hears from him hears from me and whosoever hears from me hears from Christ.

So complete upon him the chapters of the *qisma** by the brother bishops who come to you with him according to the prevailing custom. (40) Let him be given his rights and dues in order that he may be without care and may become free to pray and to intercede on their behalf by night and day, and may teach them the salvation of their souls. For the Holy Gospel says that 'the labourer is deserving of his food'.[1] And Paul the Apostle says 'Who pastures sheep and does not eat from the milk of his flock, and who plants vines and does not eat of their fruit?'[2] And he said also 'If we have sown in you spiritual things, is it a great matter to reap the bodily things?'[3] For God has summoned him as a priest over them as the Apostle says (45) 'No one will take the honour for himself except that God has summoned him like Aaron'.[4] And the Psalmist David says 'Thou art the priest for ever according to the rite of Malshîṣadâq'.[5] And we do not say this because you are deficient, rather we know that you are full of all spiritual grace, and we are ordered to remind you [of God], to teach you and to make you vigilant always. May God the Word make his coming and his reaching you to be a blessing and honour both for you and for your children, and make peace and contentment lasting in your church and in all the world, and may He save the souls of us (50) all, in order that we may offer thanks, honour and obeisance to Him [together] with His Good Father and the Holy Spirit the Life-giver, who is made equal with Him now, at every time and for ever. Amen.

[1] Lk. 10. 7.   [2] I Cor. 9. 7.   [3] I Cor. 9. 11.   [4] Heb. 5. 4.   [5] Ps. 110. 4.

The peace of the Lord which rests upon His pure disciples and his pious saints, may it rest upon him and them, and His grace and blessing be with them. Amen.

This letter, the *sîstâdikî*, i.e. the *taqlîd*,* which is for the worthy father (55) Anbâ Tîmûthâ'us, their bishop, we have confirmed with our own handwriting and we have sent it to the brother bishops to attend his enthronement over his sees in the church in which the bishops of the see sit. Glory and thanks be to God always and for ever.

Praise be to God always and for ever.

A. Witness of Mîkhâ'îl, Bishop of Atrîb (left upper)

In the Name of God the Compassionate and the Merciful

The disciple who is poor with his sins, the least of God's creatures, Mîkhâ'îl, of the church of the Lady at Atrîb* and what [belongs] to it, attended the consecration of the holy father, the most worthy chief among the sons of his race, the priest Tîmâthâ'us the Nubian, (5) as bishop over the see of Abâkîrâs and Ibrîm of the provinces of Nubia, on the nineteenth day of Hatûr, on the blessed Sunday, in the year 1088 [in the era] of the Pious Martyrs—may God provide us with their blessings, Amen—in the great church al-Mu'allaqa in Fusṭâṭ, of Miṣr, by the Gabrielic, patriarchal, lordly, paternal, pure hand, the Patriarch of the great city of Alexandria, the Miṣrî, Ethiopian and Nubian territories, the five western cities* and what is related to that. (10) May God, with a continuing of peace and contentment, perpetuate his days for the Orthodox people in the Marcan see. Amen. Monday the twenty-seventh of Hatûr. These words have been written by Mîkhâ'îl, the scorned for his sins, who hopes for God's pardon and mercy. Praise be to God always.

B. Witness of Butrus, Bishop of Ashmûnein (right upper)

In the Name of God the Compassionate and the Merciful

The disciple who is poor with his sins, the least of God's creatures, Buṭrus, the servant of the see of the city of Ashmûnein and what [belongs] to it, attended the consecration of the holy father, the most worthy chief among the sons of his race, the priest (5) Tîmâthâ'us the Nubian, as bishop over the see of Abakîrâs and Ibrîm of the provinces of Nubia, on the nineteenth day of Hatûr, on the blessed Sunday, in the year 1088 [in the era] of the Pious Martyrs, in the great church at Fusṭâṭ of Miṣr, by the Gabrielic, patriarchal, lordly, paternal, pure hand, the Patriarch of (10) the great city of Alexandria, the Miṣrî, Ethiopian and Nubian territories, the five western cities* and what is related to that. May God, [with a continuing of] peace and contentment, perpetuate his days for the Orthodox people in the Marcan see. Amen. Monday the twenty-seventh of Hatûr in the year 1088, (15) may God provide us with their (i.e. the Martyrs') blessings. Amen. These words have been written by Buṭrus, the scorned for his sins, who hopes for God's pardon and mercy. Praise be to God always.

C. Witness of Murqus, Bishop of Qifṭ (right lower)

I, the scorned for my crimes, the wretched with my sins, the most scorned of mankind, Murqus, the slave of the slave of Christ, the servant of the see of Qifṭ and what is related to it, east and west, by the grace of God and His inscrutable judgements, who raises up the poor man from the dung-heap and seats him among the heads of his people—and at this time entrusted with representing the Gabrielic, patriarchal, paternal, lordly, served *qillâya** may God perpetuate its existence [with the survival of] its possessor and may He provide all (5) with the blessing of the prayers of its incumbent, Amen—[I] attended the enthronement of the blessed, pure lord and father, the bodily angel and spiritual man, the honoured bishop Anbâ Ṭîmâthâ'us, bishop of the see of Abûkhirâs and Ibrîm and what belongs to it, in [accordance with] custom and publicly. And I have taken part in the above-mentioned, blessed enthronement and the laying of hands and the [threefold cry of] 'worthy'* with the pure father and lord, the skilled teacher, the upright pastor, the successful merchant, the honoured bishop Anbâ Athanâsyûs, bishop of the see of the city of Qûs (10) and what is related to it, east and west, and the deputy in charge of the see of the city of Armant—may God perpetuate his existence—in the church of the noble martyr Mâr Buqṭur (Victor), [at his monastery] known as Dayr al-Kûla, at the mountain of B.shûlû in the *ḥâjir* west of Qamûla,* that being on the second Sunday of the holy fast, the twentieth of Amshîr in the year 1088 [in the era] of the Pure Martyrs, may God provide us with their blessings. Amen. Praise be to God always and for ever.

D. Witness of Athanâsyûs, Bishop of Qûs (left lower)

God the Good in His Kindness

I, the scorned for my crimes, the wretched with my sins, the most scorned of mankind, Athanâsyûs, the slave of the slave of Christ and their servant in the see of the guarded city of Qûs and its provinces, east and west, by the grace of God and His inscrutable judgements, who raises up the poor man from the dungheap and seats him among the heads of his people—and at this time entrusted with representing the Gabrielic, (5) patriarchal, paternal, lordly, served *qillâya** may God perpetuate its existence with the survival of its possessor and may He provide all with the blessing of the prayers of its incumbent, Amen—[and] in charge of the see of the city of Armant and what is related to it, east and west—just as it was also in the Pauline, patriarchal, lordly, paternal days, which support that clean pure soul in eternal rest in the shining places—by the will of God, exalted is He, [I] attended the enthronement of the blessed, pure lord and father, the bodily angel and spiritual man, the honoured bishop Anbâ Ṭîmâthâ'us, bishop of the see of Abûkhirâs (10) and Ibrîm and what belongs to it, in [accordance with] custom and publicly. And I have taken part in the above-mentioned, blessed enthronement and the laying of hands and the [threefold cry of] 'worthy'* with the pure father and lord, the skilled teacher, the upright pastor, the successful merchant, the honoured bishop Anbâ Murqus, bishop of the see of the city of Qifṭ and what is related to it, east and west, and the deputy in charge of the see of the city of Dandara and what is related to it, east and west—may God perpetuate his existence—in the church of the noble martyr Mâr Buqṭur (Victor), at his monastery known as Dayr al-Kûla, at the mountain of B.shûlû in the (15) *ḥâjir* west of Qamûla,* that being on the second Sunday of the holy fast, the twentieth of Amshîr in the year 1088 [in the era] of the Pure Martyrs, may God provide us with their blessings. Amen.

Praise be to God always and eternally.

Notes on the English Translation of the Arabic Scroll

Line 8: arkhan pl. *arâkhina* <ἄρχων (see G. Graf, *Verzeichnis arabischer kirchlicher Termini*, 2nd, enlarged edn. [Corpus Scriptorum Christianorum Orientalium, vol. 147, Subsidia, tome 8]. (Louvain, 1954), p. 6).

Line 24: aqsamâhu aghûmunus^{an}. On *aqsama*, cf. Graf, op. cit. 90 and see the note on *qisma* at line 39 below. The rank *aghûmunus* (also *qummuṣ*) < ἡγούμενος (see Graf, op. cit. 10).

Line 26: al-muʻallaqa—see above, p. 22, note on line 71.

Lines 29–30: al-ʻukkâz al-jadîd—cf. above, p. 22, note on line 83; 'rod of iron' would be *ʻukkâz al-ḥadîd*.

Line 36: al-abusṭuliyya.

Line 39: al-qisma—see Graf, op. cit. 90-1, and Crum, *Coptic Dictionary*, 279; the term refers to the combination of the procedures of consecration (*takrîz*) and enthronement (*tajlîs*).

Line 54: al-sîstâdikî ay al-taqlîd—see above, p. 4.

A, line 6: see above, p. 23, note on A, line 6.

A, line 9: i.e. Pentapolis—see above, p. 22, notes on lines 19 and 20.

B, line 11: see note immediately above.

C, line 3: *qillâya* < ~~ꭩ~~ < κελλίον, κέλλα (see Graf, op. cit. 92, and above, p. 23, note on line 71). The term refers to the residence of the Patriarch at Fusṭâṭ (see D. T. A. Evetts, *The Churches and Monasteries of Egypt ... attributed to Abû Ṣâliḥ, the Armenian* (Oxford, 1895), p. 23, fn. 2 and (citing al-Maqrîzî), p. 305), and hence to the institution of Patriarch.

C, line 8: *al-aksiyûs* < ἄξιος This is the calling out of the word three times near the end of the ceremony by all present (see, for example, O. H. E. KHS-Burmester, *The Egyptian or Coptic Church* (Cairo, 1967), p. 173).

C, line 11: *kanîsat . . . mâr buqṭur [bi-dayrihi] al-maʻrûf bi-dayr al-kûla bi-jabal b.shûlû bi-ḥâjir gharb qamûla*—cf. above, pp. 20, 21, 27. The *Church of Mâr Buqṭur* at Qamûla is mentioned in the work attributed to Abû Ṣâliḥ (see Evetts, op. cit., fol. 104a) and there are now two sites, 2 km. apart, called Dayr Mârî Buqṭur (see *Survey of Egypt*, 1:25,000, map 34/780,795 (Khuzam), published in 1943; cf. O. Meinardus, *Areas of Christian Sites in Egypt* (Cairo, 1962), map III). The name *Dayr al-Kûla* is mentioned neither by al-Maqrîzî nor in the work attributed to Abû Ṣâliḥ, and appears not to have survived. The significance of *b.shûlû* is unclear: possibly a place-name; a settlement by the name of Najaʻ Bishlâw exists in the western part of the Qamûla district (see map cited), to the west of the two sites of Dayr Mârî Buqṭur by 3·5 and 4·5 km. respectively. The term *ḥâjir* can mean 'high land or ground, the middle of which is depressed' (E. W. Lane, *Arabic–English Lexicon* (London, 1863–93), sub *ḥ.j.r.*).

D, line 3: see above, note on C, line 3.

D, line 11: see above, note on C, line 8.

D, lines 14–15: see above, note on C, line 11.

PART 4

THE CALENDAR

THE CALENDAR

(PLATE XXIV)

ON the back of the Arabic Scroll, about 20 cm. below the top edge, are the remains of seven lines of numerals and abbreviations. The purpose of this entry is the compilation of a rough reckoning of the date of the Sunday before the beginning of the Lenten Fast and the date of Easter Day for the years A.D. 1372–8 inclusive. It is not altogether unlikely that this table of reckoning was the work of Bishop Timotheos himself. Certainly, if conditions in Nubia were in a disturbed state and communications with Egypt difficult, it would have been prudent for Timotheos to have the dates of the Fast and Easter calculated for at least a few years in advance of his journey to Nubia to his See.

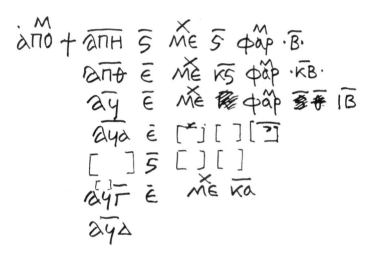

Era of the Martyrs	Epagomenal days at end of previous year	Sunday before Fast		Easter	
		Month	Day	Month	Day
1088	6	Mechir	6	Pharmouthi	2
1089	5	Mechir	26	Pharmouthi	22
1090	5	Mechir	?	Pharmouthi	? ? 12
1091	5	(Mechir)	?	?	no entry
[1092]	6	(Mechir)	?	no entry	no entry
1093	5	Mechir	21	no entry	no entry
1094	no entry	no entry	no entry	no entry	no entry

The accuracy of the dates in the first line is confirmed by the date of Timotheos' enthronement given in the witness autographs of the Bishops of Qifṭ and Qûṣ. They record that this occurred on the 20th day of Mechir A.D. 1372 which was the second Sunday in the period of the Lenten Fast. Since the Lenten Fast lasted for fifty-five days and commenced on a Monday, the date of the Sunday before the Monday in the year A.D. 1372 fell on the 6th of Mechir, which tallies exactly with the first date in the reckoning on the Scroll. The second line of dates would also appear to be correct. In the third line Bishop Timotheos, if he was the writer, fell into some difficulty, for the

41

figures after both months were obliterated. At the end of the line the figure 12 appears, but it is not clear to which month this refers. If the number is to be associated with the date of the Sunday before the Monday on which the Lenten Fast began then Easter Day would fall on 8th Pharmouthi, whereas in fact in that year it fell on the 7th. It is difficult to see under the obliterations any number other than 6 or 9. In line 4 sufficient traces remain to suggest reading Mechir, but reference to the table of actual dates, set out below, shows that this should be Phamenoth. It is possible that the Bishop wrote Mechir automatically. Judging by the number of uncompleted entries in the last four lines, it would seem that he first wrote down in a column the seven year-dates, and followed with a column giving the number of epagomenal days. Next he wrote down in column the month in which the Sunday before the Fast fell. The facts that he obliterated the numerals referring to the months in l. 3, and made no entries for the date of Easter in the lines which refer to the years 1091–4, show that he gave up the task of calculating at this point. Probably he intended to complete the calendar, seeing that it had been begun on the back of one of his Letters Testimonial which he was to present in due course to his people in Ibrîm. The circumstances which prevented him from carrying out his intention will probably never be known; but it was an incomplete calendar that he eventually carried into Nubia.

Actual dates

Year	Sunday before the Fast	Easter
1088 = 1372 A.D.	Mechir 6	Pharmouthi 2
1089 = 1373 A.D.	Mechir 26	Pharmouthi 22
1090 = 1374 A.D.	Mechir 11	Pharmouthi 7
1091 = 1375 A.D.	Phamenoth 1	Pharmouthi 27
1092 = 1376 A.D.	Mechir 22	Pharmouthi 18
1093 = 1377 A.D.	Mechir 7	Pharmouthi 3
1094 = 1378 A.D.	Mechir 27	Pharmouthi 23

THE PLATES

NOTE ON THE PLATES

THE photographs for Pls. I–IV, XIV, XXIV, were taken by me on Ilford Pan F 35 mm. Gevaert Negative Colour 35 mm. was used for the remainder. The fact that the Scrolls, after their unrolling, had been placed under glass in large wooden frames presented problems in making adequate photographic records. Removal of the glass would have been difficult and almost certainly unwise in view of the brittle nature of the paper upon which the documents had been written. In December 1965 the authorities at the Egyptian Museum in Cairo very kindly arranged for the Scrolls to be recorded on a larger format camera by their official photographers, but unfortunately the only film then obtainable proved to be quite unsatisfactory for the purpose.   J. M. P.

PLATE I

BLOCKED ENTRANCE TO THE NORTH CRYPT

PLATE II

BURIAL OF BISHOP TIMOTHEOS UNDER ENTRANCE TO
THE NORTH CRYPT

PLATE III

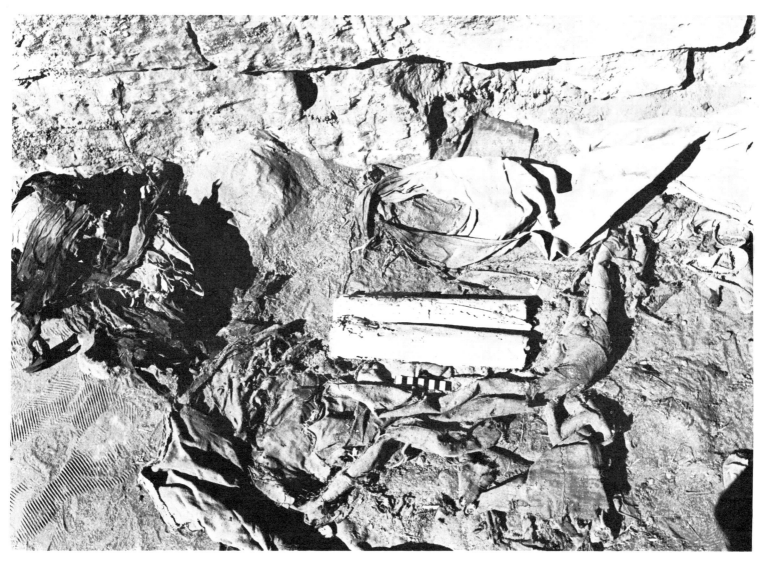

SCROLLS AS FOUND UNDER THE BODY OF THE BISHOP

PLATE IV

THE COPTIC SCROLL UNROLLED IN THE LABORATORY OF
THE EGYPTIAN MUSEUM, CAIRO

PLATE V

THE COPTIC SCROLL
ll. 1–4

PLATE VI

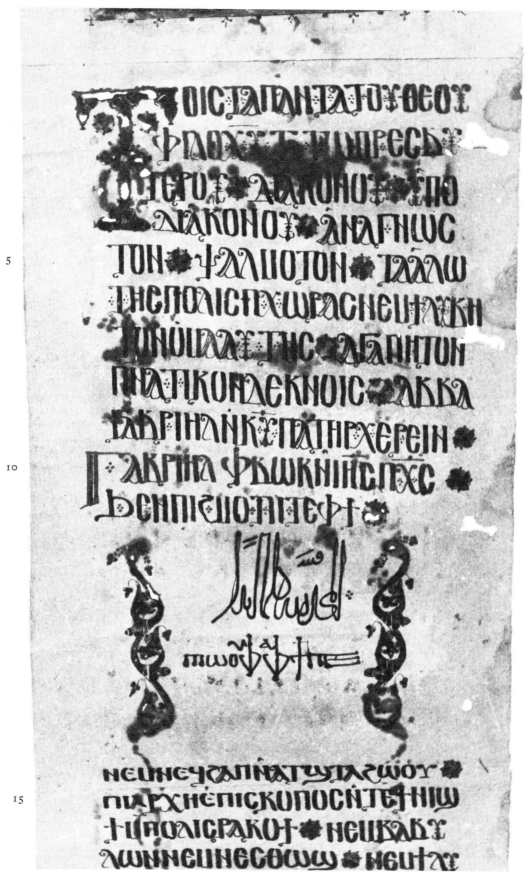

THE COPTIC SCROLL

ll. 1–17

PLATE VII

15

20

25

30

35

40

45

THE COPTIC SCROLL
ll. 14–47

PLATE VIII

THE COPTIC SCROLL

ll. 44–73

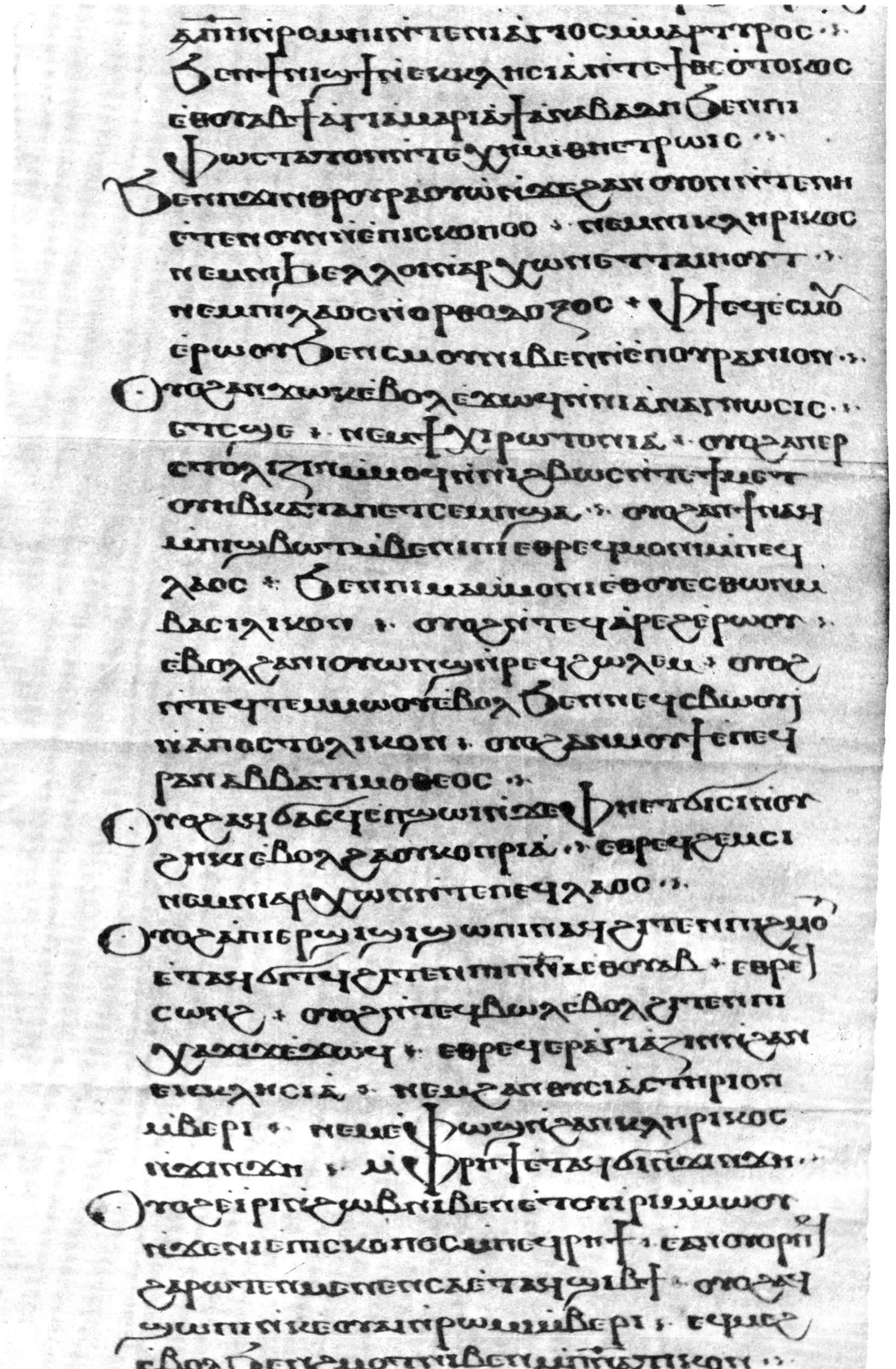

THE COPTIC SCROLL
ll. 70–104

PLATE X

105

110

115

120

125

130

135

140

THE COPTIC SCROLL

ll. 102–141

PLATE XI

THE COPTIC SCROLL
ll. 139–175

PLATE XII

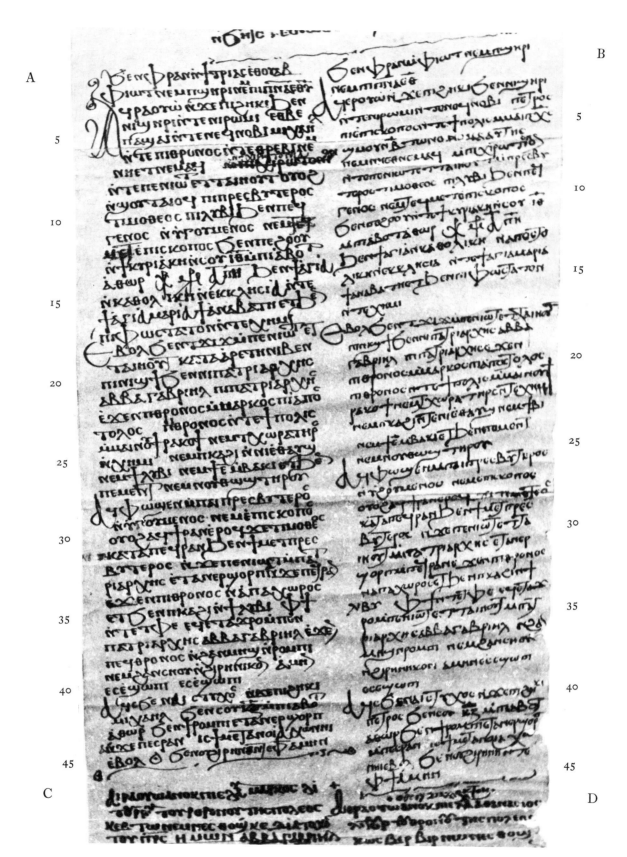

THE COPTIC SCROLL

Witness texts: A, ll. 1a–45a
B, ll. 1b–45b
C, ll. 1c–4c
D, ll. 1d–4d

PLATE XIII

THE COPTIC SCROLL

Witness texts: A, ll. 43a–45a
B, ll. 42b–45b
C, ll. 1c–32c
D, ll. 1d–38d
The Greek Postscript (bottom, right)

PLATE XIV

THE COPTIC SCROLL

The Greek Postscript

PLATE XV

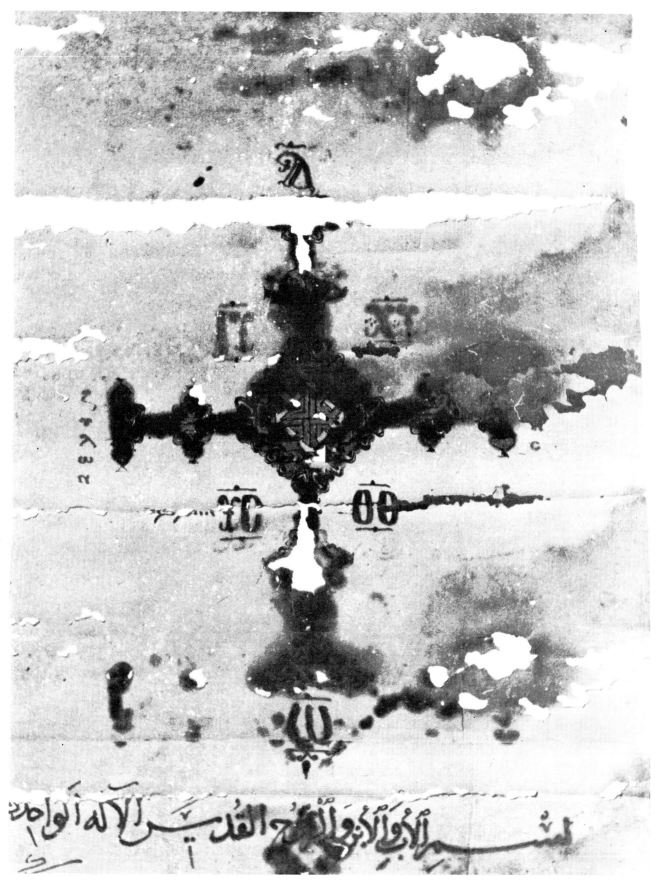

THE ARABIC SCROLL

l. 1

PLATE XVI

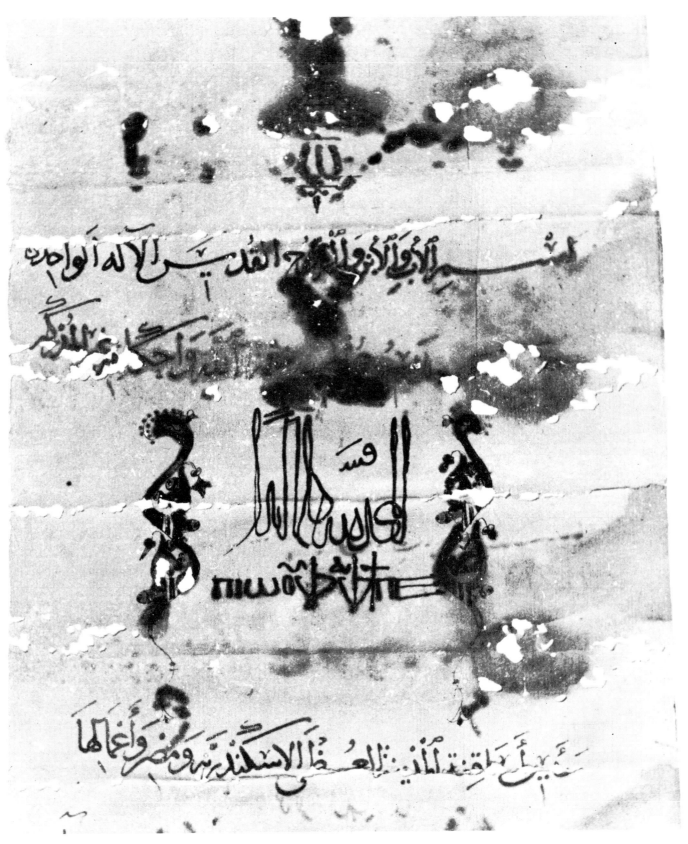

THE ARABIC SCROLL

ll. 1–5

PLATE XVII

5

10

THE ARABIC SCROLL

ll. 5–11

PLATE XVIII

THE ARABIC SCROLL

ll. 11–17

PLATE XIX

والساعر فنی الاعطی الرسول وجمع العاد سر امری

اطالما اراد الرسل بر ید عوالهم اسمعه الحوصل کر اسا اناسوس

الاثقو کان بح اسد عسه مرار جار الاح الحد

العاما الحمد للمسح الصالح الودبع المواضع المعری

صاحب العلد السلم والروح المسمعه الاسطراس

الماسی فی مرصاد الساعی وسلسله الممدوح السره البعی السسروره

الملوایا موسا ویدایا الاریادکسی الراهب العسل الکرم طمو یاوس

مراجل الة مستحقا هذه الریاسه اقتمناه اعومنا و کلناه استقناعاد الکلای

المقدم دکلا یوم الاحد یاسع عشر هتور سنة تمایه و تمابر والفب المنهد الخطاد

THE ARABIC SCROLL

ll. 17–25

PLATE XX

25

المتقدم ذكره واليوم الاحد تاسع عشر شهر توت سنة ثمانيه وقماير والف للشهداء الاطهار

في الكنيسه الكبرى التي للستي الطاهره مرتمرم البتول المعلقه بمصر قاه

30

مصر المحروسه لحضور بعض الاساقفه والكهنه والشيوخ الاجلا الاراخنه و

الاربعه في الرب بارك عليهم بكل البركات السمايه وطاعه عليه الصلوات

اللايقه بالتكرر والبهاء الثياب الكهنوتيه كاجب واعطينا الاحكام

الجديد ليرع شعبه والمرج الخصيب الملوكي ولحفظهم من الذياب الخاطفه

بمحضر المعالم الاتوليه وحضرنا ابنها طيبا تاوس كان اولاد ووضعه الـ

يرفع الفقير من الاب المجلس مع رووسا شعبه وصاره السلطان من قبل النعمه

التي نالها امر الروح القدس بوضع اليد ان يجاور يربط ويكرز الحاضر والهياكل الجدد

وقسم الكنيسه جعانا اجا الطب ايا وجعل جميع ما اعله الاساقفه امثاله واسلاه النـ

الكرم من بعد ما نتلد صار السنا جديد ملوا مر كل حكمه ونعمه زوجانه من نبل النعمه

35

THE ARABIC SCROLL

ll. 25–35

PLATE XXI

الننى

اليكم من بعد ما تبتلوا صابرًا جلدًا جلوا مركل حلمه ونعمه روحانيه من نبل النعم 35

فتقبلوا

ناكها والدرجة لابد طالبه التي تسلمها وصارتاليه   مبثوثه لهم ونجب عليهم ان

كاصرالله

ويعملوا باكرايم وفرح وابتهاج وخضوع وان يسمعوا الاسمه كلامه لاشتد لك

والمعلم الصالح فمن سمع منه فقد سمع منى ومن سمع منى فقد سمع من المسيح فليعملوا به

ــ

الفصول   التي للقسه على يدى الاخوه الاساقفه الواصلين اليكم معه جارى احاه

في

ولبعض حقوقه ورسومه حتى يكون غير اهمال ويصير مشرفًا للصلاه والطلبه عنهم 40

اللبل والنهار ويسلم خلاص نفوسهم   لان جيل المقدس يقول ان الاجير مستحق لطعامه

ويقول ايضا من يتعب من القول من الاى يرعى غنما ولا ياكل من لبن رعيته   او من الاى يكرم

كرمًا ولا ياكل من تمره وقال ايضا انما قدر عنا فيكم التوجابا

اعظيم يهوان يحصد فيكم الجسد الباث   لان الادعاه لاهنا عليهم كما يقول الرسول 45

اطلبا اجل ياحل الكرامه لغته الاى لعون الله مسامح ويقول ايضا المزار اوودبار

PLATE XXII

تلك انتاكام الملك البدع على طقوسه ملكيصدق ولم تعمل هذا ولاكنكم ناقصون بل نحن نعم

انكم ممتليون من كل نعمة روحانيه وقلنا امرنا ان ذكركم ووعكم وبقطكم دايا

والله الكلمة جعل محبته ووصوله اليكم يكون بالهيكة والكرامه عليكم قيم دوادكم

وتجعل السلامه والطمانينه دايمة في بعتكم وروكل المسكونه وخلق نفوسنا

جمعا المقدم له الشكر والكرامه والجود مع ابيه الصالح والروح القدس المحيى المساوي

معه الان وكل اوان والى دهر الداهرين امين ٥

سلام الزمان الحال على بلامده الاطهار وقد يسسه الابرار حال علمه

وعليهم ونعمته وبركته يكون معهم امين

مده الرساله السينطادكي اي التقليد الدي لاب الفاضل

ابا طومانا ورسى استقفهم مناكما حظ اليها واحتكها الى الاخوه الانافقه لبحضروا لجلسه على المنيه في البيعه النبي

بجلس فيها الساقفه الكربى ٥ والمجد والشكر لله دايا ليداه

سلم الاب وعمه للرحم والشهرير للاب بسم الاب الى نفف الرحيم انك

THE ARABIC SCROLL

ll. 46–58

PLATE XXIII

A

B

D

C

THE ARABIC SCROLL

Witness texts

PLATE XXIV

THE CALENDAR ON THE VERSO OF THE ARABIC SCROLL